Heroes of
HOT RODDING

David Fetherston

Motorbooks International
Publishers & Wholesalers ®

This book is dedicated to my father
Gerald Henry Fetherston,
who told me
late-night tales
of hot rod Fords.

First published in 1992 by Motorbooks
International Publishers & Wholesalers, P O Box 2,
729 Prospect Avenue, Osceola, WI 54020 USA

Library of Congress Cataloging-in-Publication
Data
Fetherston, David A.
    Heroes of hot rodding / David A. Fetherston.
        p.   cm.
    Includes index.
    ISBN 0-87938-384-4
    1. Automobile racing drivers—United
States—Biography.
I. Title.
GV1032.A1F43 1992
796.7'2'092—dc20   91–33574
[B]

On the front cover: *Dennis and Debbie Kyle's "stroker"*
1932 Ford roadster on the Bonneville Salt Flats. With its
292 ci Chevy V–8, it runs the quarter mile in 13.04
seconds at 104 mph. Fetherston/Russell
Insets: *Tommy Ivo (left) and Dean Moon (right).*

On the back cover: *Jerry and Karel Helwig's 1940*
coupe, first modified in the 1950s by the Boyd Brothers
in Oregon, has a Kinsler fuel-injected 270 ci V–8 90
flathead. It has run 119.6 mph at Bonneville in the 1990s.
Fetherston/Russell

Printed and bound in the United States of America

Contents

Preface

Hot rodding has become an international mode of communication. It has transcended the barriers of class, race and creed while binding people from around the world into an enormous community simply known as "hot rodders."

Heroes of Hot Rodding is my attempt to put a small part of American automotive history into perspective. I have tried to capture the spirit and character of many of hot rodding's most famous characters so we may all enjoy and appreciate these folks a little more. Each chapter is dedicated to a hot rodding personality and could be its own book.

There are many stories told about hot rodding's early days. I hope we have added to those tales while getting most dates correct. Many other individuals have contributed greatly to the sport of hot rodding, but time, space and availability have not allowed me to pursue each and every one.

My view of hot rodding's "roots" includes not only the dry lakes racers, the drag racers, the performance parts guys, the street rodders and Bonneville, but also the custom car builders, the organizers, the pinstripers and the kit car dreamers, all of whom helped unfold the history of the sport.

I started this project because I could not find reference to these pioneers of hot rodding when I was researching my stories as an automotive journalist. I have tried to cover most bases so that you'll get to know these people a little more clearly.

I would like to thank all those who graciously gave their time and contributed their photos. In particular, I would like to remember the help that Dean and Shirley Moon gave me in getting the project under way. I would also like to thank Dave Wallace for his wonderfully timed help, John Lawlor for his assistance with the chapter on Mickey Thompson, Ron Moorehead for his help with Jocko, Mike Chase for his help with captions, Greg Williams for his continual encouragement and Don Russel for his superb printing of the photography.

For me, the best part of this book was not in finishing it; my hot rod heroes are now my friends. I thank my partner Gloria for her forbearance in helping *Heroes of Hot Rodding* grow from a seed into a tribute to hot rodding's pioneers.

David Fetherston

Chapter 1

Joe Bailon

Many of hot rodding's founding fathers had to endure lean years of little luxury and sometimes barely enough sustenance in the twenties and thirties. Those grim Depression years left young Americans determined to make their adult lives comfortable and enjoyable. The attractive freedom and exhilarating speed of automobiles were particularly appealing because they were such a far cry from the broken-down cars and mundane work trucks that provided Depression-era transportation.

Joe Bailon, the youngest of ten children in a migrant farm worker family, spent his youth either on those broken-down vehicles or working in the dusty central-California fields to which they carried him. Those rusty, dusty farm trucks cast a black-and-white pall over his childhood, yet he nurtured a young boy's rich imagination, one which probably envisioned the wonderful world of color he would one day create.

His family toiled as field workers and the Depression forced them to take young Joe out of school, just as he finished second grade, to help the family pick and pack fruit. They were paid ten cents an hour. Joe spent his free time creating small toys out of the wooden off-cuts from the packing case factory. He would nail and whittle small cars and trucks and, with this focus on cars and trucks, he dreamed of owning one.

Joe turned sixteen in 1938 and bought his first car. He bought a 1929 Model A Ford coupe and proceeded to swap the coupe body at a local scrap yard for a cabriolet body. He took it home and in a short time had chopped off the soft top. He added mirrors, horns and lights, then hand-painted the tires with whitewalls.

One additional feature completed the car: a flamed paint job over the nose. His custom "A" was the first recorded vehicle with a flame paint job. This "A" started the custom car craze and Joe's voyage into the world of beautiful hand-built automobiles had begun.

In the best biographical story tradition, life never runs smoothly and events influence and shape a man's character. World War II soon had Joe working in a shipbuilding yard in Hayward, California. He learned the skills of a torch cutter and used a gas torch to cut out complex shapes from thick plates of steel used in war and cargo ships. In 1943, he was drafted into the military and served the last two years of the war in the Army. Those years taught him many new skills but he knew he had a certain direc-

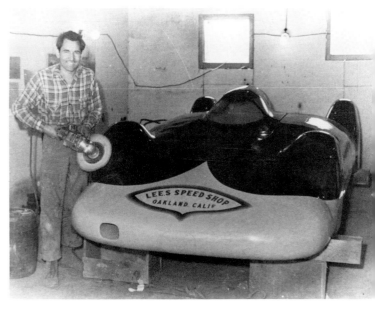

Joe buffed out the Lee's Speed Shop Bonneville streamliner in his shop in Oakland in 1954.

Joe's most famous creation, Miss Elegance, is shown while still in her "suede" finish. The car was a seven-year project, and the finished product bore little resemblance to the 1941 coupe from which it was developed. Note the wonderfully low gas prices. No wonder early hot rodders thought nothing of cruising all night.

tion in life, and custom automobiles were in there somewhere.

After Joe was discharged, he bought a 1938 Ford three-window coupe. He had seen others customize their cars, and one in particular, Tommy the Greek, had a 1940 Merc' with a chopped Carson top, a lowering job and trick body work. Joe liked his ideas, but he had some of his own and he started redoing his 1938 Ford. Using only his common sense and excellent craftsman skills, Joe lowered the Ford, dropped new taillights into the rear fenders and set the license plate into the trunk.

The coupe looked stylish with its lines cleaned up a touch. Joe's work impressed a local paint and

Polished and toothy, Miss Elegance, Joe's famous 1941 Chevy coupe. It met a sad end, however, apparently being crushed in the midst of a divorce settlement because the couple could not agree on who would get the car.

fender shop and he was hired as its body building specialist and customizer. When Joe finished his 1938 Ford coupe, a customer in the shop admired the Ford with its beautiful maroon-ruby finish. He promptly offered Joe $700 for the car—to which Joe casually agreed, as it had cost him only $250. This gave him enough money to start on his next custom car venture, a 1941 Chevy club coupe. It became the first car for which the name "Joe Bailon" was noted.

The Chevy coupe turned out to be a seven-year project. "Miss Elegance" was the result: the full-bodied, high-riding coupe was turned into a low, smooth and graceful custom car. The fenders were molded and filled, the hood was shaved, the top was chopped and all original trim was removed. Joe built a new all-molded nose and a new grille and sank the headlights into the front of the car, where they had originally protruded in bomb-like mounts.

The dash was just as exotic, with sixteen gauges and a multitude of switches and chrome. Joe had restyled everything on the car, leaving very little to resemble the 1941 coupe's stock appearance.

Joe finished off Miss Elegance with a paint finish of a quality never seen before. It had a deep gloss to its brown-maroon color that astounded everyone who saw it. During the developing of Miss Elegance, Joe relocated, and the car was finally completed in 1952 at his Haywood shop in the San Francisco Bay Area.

Miss Elegance received an outstanding reception at her first public showing, winning "The Most Elegant" award at the Oakland Roadster Show, the first of numerous prizes won at West Coast shows.

In later years, Joe spent a considerable time searching for Miss Elegance, hoping to buy her back. Unhappily, he discovered that the car had been torn apart, the parts sold and the body crushed. The poor old car had been caught up in the middle of a divorce settlement and the owner had decided that if he couldn't keep her, there was no way his wife was going to have her either!

Miss Elegance's winnings drew many customers to Joe's Hayward shop, which was suddenly a mini boom-town for custom cars. He employed several people at the shop but only as helpers to strip the cars down for him to do his work. He did all of the trick work himself, with his assistants spreading the lead, hand sanding and preparing the car.

This became the system Joe used to build more than 500 cars at his Hayward workshop. Cars were chopped, channeled and sectioned. Convertibles were turned into hardtops and fins, scoops and skirts were added. Fords, Mercurys, Chevys, Oldsmobiles and Pontiacs were on the menu and Bailon was the head chef. As chef, Joe had another treat to serve up to the unsuspecting automotive world: Candy Apple Paints.

Joe became a master of the spray gun and is renowned for his amazing gloss finishes. For many years he strived to blend a paint that was strong in color, had a deep lustre and was translucent. One day when he was blending a paint batch, he spilt two colors on a bench surface—and there was the look he wanted. He had accidentally blended a gold with red—and the very first Candy Apple Red was running all over his bench!

He and his wife Marie worked on the idea, blending up more amazing colors using this technique (not spilling them all over the bench but using a scientific mixing system). The result was a full range of Candy Apple colors from Red to Wild Cherry, Tangerine to Orchid Pink.

Joe's next fifteen years were dedicated to building hundreds of customs until he decided to go south and attack the southern California market. He moved to North Hollywood, where his style of work changed. He began customizing late-model cars. His name was well known by this time and movie stars began calling, all wanting the Bailon touch.

Zsa Zsa Gabor had Joe customize her Roller with thirties-style headlights and a restyled body. Sammy Davis, Jr., had Joe build a Chevy Vega Wagon with wood panels on the sides and a custom

front, a Roller-style grille and wire wheels. Dean Martin had him put together a Cadillac station wagon, and James Garner had Joe do family-car body repairs.

Hollywood studios commissioned him, too. Jay Ohrberg hired Joe to build the Pink Panther car, which looks like a cross between a pink hairbrush and an anteater. The Pink Panther has an Oldsmobile front-wheel-drive chassis as its basis, and is a show car that has been used in several movies, TV shows and commercials. Exotic and colorful, it uses round and square tubes, and measures twenty-four feet.

Another project was the Snakepit, which looked like two coffins mounted side-by-side. Under the hoods were six V-8 engines with a "snakepit" packed with forty-eight exhaust headers. Other custom jobs followed. Joe built cars for George Barris, who put the Barris name on them as the builder and not the designer, a very sore point with Joe. During this time, he also built the Tall T and the Barber Chair hot rods.

Joe's work turned him into a living legend of the custom car and hot rod fraternity. One of his customs is on permanent exhibition at the Oakland Museum

Here's a look at the incredible dash of Miss Elegance, which was loaded with all the bells and whistles. It seemed to have as many dials, gauges, controls, buttons and knobs as an airplane cockpit, an impression enhanced by the fact that actual controls were reflected in the chrome steering column.

Here's Joe, circa 1990, with the immense dash he recovered from the crushed Miss Elegance.

of Modern Art. It is a scalloped and customized coupe called "The Mystery Ford." It is finished in red and gold, has wide whites and has chrome reverse rims, another of Joe's inventions.

He entered five cars in the Oakland Roadster Show in 1956, all fitted with chrome reverse rims. He recalled that he didn't even get a kiss for that idea, but within twelve months, chrome reverse wheels were all the rage.

Bullets, which are pointed chrome tips that fit anything they can be screwed or welded to, are another Bailon first. They were made up in all sizes and used in grilles, dashes and hubcaps.

Joe continued to be inventive. He discovered that electrical conduit could be molded onto flat surfaces to create designs and was just the right product to frame up grille cavities and wheel wells.

The list goes on; he is the master tactition of custom car construction. Joe, the Candy Man, stylishly rolled more than 1,000 custom cars out the doors of his workshop.

Joe has now slowed to a comfortable pace as he lives in Auburn, California, not far from the prune and grape farms where he began to dream of great things. Behind his house is a long row of garages containing at least five restoration jobs or new customs. Other projects include the completion of the four leadsleds in his driveway, the restoration of three of his earlier customs for himself, and the construction of "Miss Elegance II."

At 70 years of age, Joe is cruising at his own speed. Judging by what he has accomplished in the past few years and what he is building at the

Spence Murray pulls up and pauses in his custom 1936 Ford roadster, a creation of Joe's. It featured a LaSalle grille, skirts and a gorgeous red paint job.

Long and low, this is a beautiful 1950 Ford custom done up in red and white, a favorite color scheme of Joe's, one that fit the hot, moving image of his creations.

The rich back end of "Scoopee," Joe's famous 1958 Chevy custom coupe. Your eye couldn't scan a foot of the car without encountering some sign of his customizing handiwork.

The layered, sculpted side of Joe's work shows through in this Mercury custom from the fifties.

moment, he will continue to run in overdrive for years to come. Clients from all over the United States still seek him out. At the base of the Sierra Nevada mountains in Auburn, Joe works far from the hustle and madness that he found in Hollywood. As Joe said, "People are crazy down there! Up here, I can build cars the way I want."

Joe's pet peeve is that credit for a car shouldn't just be given to the designer but to the builder also—a point overlooked so many times in the past as many of his cars were credited to other showman car builders.

The walls of his den are covered with mementos of past victories. One wall has more than thirty *Rod and Custom* magazine covers featuring vehicles he made in the fifties and sixties. Another is a plaque from the West Coast Cruise organization, which says, "Presented to Joe Bailon. A very special thanks. You will always be Number One to all of us." With a salute like that from his peers, it's easy to see why Joe Bailon is called the "King of Customs."

The famous "El Gato" was a car Joe built for Ford's touring car show exhibit. It was built around a 1970 Mercury Cougar.

Chapter 2

Craig Breedlove

Norman Craig Breedlove was always ahead of his time. He owned and drove his first cars while still under legal age, and he possessed mechanical knowledge and skills that were always well beyond his years. He even seemed to try to cheat time by rocketing at such great speeds in his Land Speed

Craig had the look of (and almost as much speed as) a dashing astronaut as he strode from the Sonic 1, which was designed to break the sound barrier. It eventually ran 600.6 mph in 1965, giving Craig a record that stood for the next six years.

Craig is shown in 1963 as he geared up for his most successful record attempts. With movie-star looks and more speed than anyone in the world, he became an international celebrity.

Record vehicles that he might break not only the sound barrier but also the time barrier. It was fitting that his famous speed runs came in the sixties, an era in which U.S. culture moved and changed at an alarmingly rapid rate. In many ways, Breedlove the driver was as deserving of the title of "Spirit of America" as were his speed machines.

His perception of speed was first formed when he was eight years old and built powered model airplanes that he flew with a local club. Soon, he was engaged in stunt flying and subsequently won many contests flying his wire-controlled aircraft. He had an eye for fabrication and by age ten was scratch-building his own models. He rapidly became a junior expert in aerodynamics.

Across the road from his home in Mar Vista, California, lived the Rourke family. Son number one, Roger, had a hot rod. It looked, sounded and smelled awfully good to young Breedlove, who was fascinated with anything with a motor. He often tinkered about over at his neighbor's place, shoe-horning in on any information that passed between the hot rodders.

Craig was an undaunted worker. From the age of nine, he held an after-school job and, as cars became his prime interest, he took on a new after-

Engineers worked on the front wheel of the Spirit of America just before its 526-mph record run in 1964. Note that the team crew's jackets bear Craig's old record of 428.37 mph, a mark he set in 1963.

Here's a rear view of the Spirit of America with its immense vertical stabilizer.

school job sanding cars at a local body shop for fifty cents an hour. He saved enough by the end of his twelfth year to buy a 1934 Ford coupe.

The five-window coupe became, instead, a family present for his thirteenth birthday, and young Breedlove was delighted. He immediately started building his first car into a classic California hot rod. It was not going to be just another decked-over car, but would be a chopped and channeled racer powered by a blown Ford flathead.

His talent as a designer and fabricator developed as he used his drafting lessons in school to design parts and his machine shop classes to make them. Although still too young to legally drive on the street, Craig managed to get the Ford to a number of dry lakes in the Mojave Desert and hit most of the new southern Californian drag strips, picking up an armful of trophies and SCTA (Southern California Timing Association) dash tags.

Back in his garage, he removed the single, blown flathead and turned the car into a mid-mounted, twin-engined coupe. It, too, won several class records. With the Rourke brothers, he worked on a Bonneville belly tank. Weekends found him cruising with friends to the Piccadilly and Clock drive-ins to check out the new hot rods, and when he graduated from Venice High School, his highest grades were in machine shop and drafting.

He married at eighteen and by twenty-one had three children. He continued to work on his hot rods, but also had a full-time job at Douglas Aircraft as an assistant structural engineering technician, testing wing structures and landing gear. During his time at Douglas, he developed an extensive knowledge of aircraft fabrication materials and their properties.

In late 1960, he left Douglas to take a job as a fireman in Costa Mesa, California. This change allowed him the flexibility to pursue his own evolving interests. He wanted to race again but not on the dry lakes; this time he wanted to transcend hot rods and go after the world's Land Speed Record (LSR). As a child with his physics books, Craig had read of Britain's John Cobb and his triumph in achieving the speed record. It struck an inner chord that, forty years later, still rang strong. From mere dreams and thoughts, the concept of a record run developed as he worked the idea over in his mind.

One day, while on a routine call with the fire department, Craig discovered a surplus General Electric J–47 jet engine in a crate behind a ware-

In a photo that looks like it was shot on the moon, a crowd gathers around Breedlove on the Bonneville Salt Flats to celebrate two key events in October 1964: He had just set a new Land Speed Record and he had survived the crash that followed. He lost both chutes, snapped off a telegraph pole and burned his brakes before crashing over a levee and landing in a brine-filled pond.

Happy that he's alive and a record-setter, Craig sits atop the submerged Spirit of America in the pond at the Salt Flats in October 1964.

house. That routine call would forever change his life. Five-hundred dollars was the engine's asking price. Cash changed hands quickly and Craig had the core for the "world's wildest hot rod."

Craig had a clear direction and was destined for a meeting with the laws of physics. Drawing upon his storehouse of knowledge, he designed a "jet without wings." He found help with the design work from Hughes Aircraft engineer Bill Moore. Moore set the

three-wheel concept in motion and the two men came up with a low-transonic shape which they hoped would literally "fly along the ground."

Craig named the vehicle "Spirit of America," and went looking for sponsorship, and got it from Bill Lawler, one of the managers of Shell Oil Company in Santa Monica. Further searching helped him land Goodyear as the second major sponsor.

With the help of Ed Perkins, Craig set up shop in the old Perkins Battery Shop in Costa Mesa. It took two months just to scrape the old tar off the floor but once work on the speed machine got under way, it moved along briskly. The main assembly was completed and regular business at the Battery Shop slowed as the staff labored to get the Spirit of America moving along. Craig eventually moved the project to his father's home in West Los Angeles, swapping houses with his father in the process. The West L.A. house was filled with the vehicle's components. The duct work was stored in the lounge and the garage was overflowing with a rapidly growing race car.

One year later, Craig's three-wheeled LSR racer was complete. Quinn Epperly from nearby Gardena had hammered out much of the body and Craig made the rest, including the nose, air ducts and wheel flares, from fiberglass.

Craig had good luck with the static testing of his models. On weekends, he managed to gain access to the wind tunnel at the Naval Postgraduate School in Monterey, California. For six weekends, he drove up from Los Angeles to run the models through the standard testing procedures on a movable ground-plane, which was capable of moving at 1,000 feet per second. He learned a lot from this testing and modified several shapes on the car for better aerodynamic response.

During the summer of 1962, Craig took the Spirit of America to Bonneville for its first round of testing. He found plenty to test and correct. The steering system caused the Spirit to wander all over at high speeds. He tracked the problem to an incorrect steering gear ratio. At more than 150 mph, the car was designed to steer with the nose wing, which sat vertically in front of the wheel. He also discovered that the brakes were below par and that the racer had basic stability problems.

Back in Los Angeles, Craig discussed his problem with engineer friends, such as Dr. Purshing, who suggested that the design needed a large rear stabilizer in the form of a single fixed fin. This was among many design changes that were made.

In the summer of 1963, Craig returned to the Bonneville Salt Flats in Utah and tried again. The FIA (Federation Internationale de l'Automobile) was on hand to sanction his runs—after initially giving the project the thumbs down.

In the cold, clear crisp air of an August morning, Craig Breedlove stepped into the Spirit of America

Here's the Spirit of America on display at a car show in 1962, without its tail.

and shattered John Cobbs' record which had stood for sixteen years. Running at 90% throttle, Craig rocketed through the measured mile at 388.47 mph. He made his return run at 428.37 mph, giving him a two-way average of 407.45 mph.

His success turned him into an overnight international celebrity, but others were waiting to try to beat the new record. The Arfon brothers, Art and Walter, both had LSR racers. Twelve months later, Tom Green, driving Walt Arfon's "Wingfoot Express," broke the record with a speed of 413 mph. Brother Art was next. Three days later, he moved the record up to 434 mph.

Craig was motivated; he wanted the record back. The Spirit had been in the workshop all year and was upgraded with a more powerful J–47 engine, which generated 5,700 pounds of thrust. He ran the car through a series of track tests and then in mid-October 1964, Craig was ready to try to once again be the fastest man on earth. His modifications included improved hydraulic brakes, which would help launch the Spirit like a jet off a carrier so he could run it up to speed and leave the line at a much higher boost.

Using the ten-mile course, the FIA had the measured mile set four-and-a-half miles along the track. Craig's two-way average took him down and back at 485.27 mph: a new world's Land Speed Record, but not the 500 mph mark he had hoped to break.

The ride of his life was about to take place two days later. In the early morning of October 15, 1964, Craig fired up the J–47 and headed down the course. His first run gave him a speed of 513 mph. He had the engine opened out to maximum power, and the return journey was about to put him firmly back in the history books with a new record and a startling finish. He made his second run at 539.89 mph. His two-way average was 526 mph, which made Craig the first man on land through the 500–mph barrier.

This return trip must rate as one of the most amazing rides in the history of the automobile. After passing through the end of the measured mile marker, Craig released the safety parachute while still traveling in excess of 500 mph. The chute simply ripped off. The second emergency chute also ripped off.

His braking package, only good for speeds below 150 mph, did little to slow the Spirit as it

The Screaming Yellow Zonker draws some media attention, which was exactly why the speed run machine was popular with sponsors over the years.

Craig posed in appropriate leather togs with the English Leather Special, which he drove to an acceleration record of 377.75 mph in 4.65 seconds—from a standing start. This photo graced the front of a postcard Breedlove sent out to prospective customers when he worked as an agent for a Manhattan Beach, California, realty company.

wheeled on down the course. Passing the pit area and still traveling in excess of 200 mph, Craig clipped a telegraph pole, snapping it off but doing little damage to the car. What really slowed the Spirit down was a stretch of shallow water a quarter of a mile long.

Beyond the stretch of water was an eight-foot-high dike retaining a drainage area. Still unable to stop, Craig's Spirit rode over the dike and landed in a twenty-foot-deep pool. Craig recalls his first thought: "I am going to drown after running 500 mph."

He had managed to open the cockpit canopy before he crashed into the pond, which enabled him to snake out of the cockpit and float to the surface. The crash had knocked the wind out of him, but not the spirit. He swam to shore and lay resting on his stomach, laughing. His crew arrived, expecting the worst, but Craig was in high spirits, buzzing on adrenalin and pacing along the dike asking for his posted speed. Craig's famous line from the scene was caught by TV crews and beamed around the world: "For my next trick, I am going to set myself on fire." He was elated with his time, and so were the

Craig made such an international name for himself that all sorts of companies wanted him as a spokesman. Couparral snowmobiles signed him as a spokesman and celebrity driver, even building the Sno-Job speed run machine for him. It's parked alongside one of the company's consumer sleds, a Mach III.

media, which put him on the front pages of newspapers and magazine covers all over the globe.

Others were also pressing the speed envelope. Art Arfon upped the numbers and took the title away again but, undeterred, Craig returned the following year with a new jet car called "Sonic 1," which was powered by an even larger GE–79 turbojet. Goodyear was his main sponsor, contributing most of the half-million dollars that it took to build the new four-wheeled car.

Craig's shop was in Compton, California, on the edge of Watts. It was the summer of 1965 and Watts erupted into a week of riots. As the looting and burning raged on outside, Craig spent six straight days in his shop, armed with a shotgun and enough ammunition to protect himself and Sonic 1. He talked a troop of National Guard soldiers in a half track into stationing themselves in front of his shop while he kept a low-profile watch from the rooftop. "The only way these guys were going to burn my car was over my dead body," Craig recalled. The project went ahead as soon as the riots were over and was completed on schedule.

Sonic 1's first trials turned up a multitude of problems, including caved-in body sections and an engine blast that shattered the canopy and tipped Sonic 1 onto its two right wheels. Craig quickly solved these problems and was ready to run in early November 1965.

His return run after completing the first round of repairs gave him a few heart-stopping moments. Running at close to 600 mph, he discovered that Sonic 1 was trying to imitate an airplane and fly. Shutting the engine down got the nose back on the ground. He opened the chutes, but they evaporated in a whoosh of shredding energy as they were ripped from the rear of the car. Slowing to around 450 mph, Craig started applying the brakes. He eventually stopped several miles past the end of the track in a bed of soft sand—with the brake calipers fused to the discs.

His 555.12-mph two-way average on the Bonneville Salt Flats returned to him the crown and title of the fastest man on earth. His glory didn't last long. Within a month, Art Arfon had claimed the title again with a blistering 594 mph, but he destroyed his car in the process.

Craig's appetite for speed was unsated. He went back to the Salt Flats, assuring himself that Art Arfon would not gobble up the record again. His two-way

Driving this 427-powered Shelby Daytona Coupe, Craig set some FIA world endurance records on the salt.

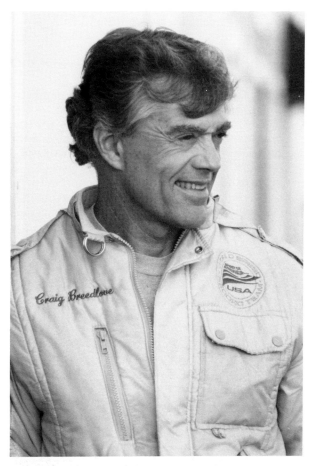

Craig Breedlove, circa 1990.

records on the Goodyear test track in Texas. These endurance races accounted for 106 new records. These wins made the AMX the hit of the Detroit Auto Show, catching Ford and Chevrolet off guard. Craig then built a streamliner powered by an American Motors V–8, but it managed just 390 mph on the Bonneville Salt Flats.

Then, just as his main card with American Motors was being played, a flood in the heart of Torrance destroyed his race car shop, ending his American Motors contract. Other facets of his life were also in turmoil. He divorced, and then found himself broke because his insurance didn't cover flood damage. For a while, he drifted around, racing cars for other people, including the English Leather rocket car and the Screaming Yellow Zonker.

But it's hard to keep a good man down, especially one of the world's most famous hot rodders. To regain control of his finances, Craig moved into real estate. It was an excellent move, as he found he had a talent for the business. He managed to involve himself in several profitable real estate ventures and built a sports complex.

Life settled into a rhythm for Craig with a new wife, Jocelyn, and he was helping his son run a Formula Ford race car. But his need for speed was not being fulfilled, so he formed "Spirit of America Enterprises." He intends to become the first man to set all three great speed records in one year—Land, Air and Water—with his "Summer of Records." All three attempts will be made with the same J–79 engine.

Craig Breedlove is in his fifties but looks like a man in his late-thirties. He was the first jet-powered racer to go 400, 500 and then 600 mph. His credentials for being the fastest man on earth are without question. The next round of racing is going to be a mind-boggling triple-header from a man whose vision of the future started with flathead Fords on the dry lakes of southern California.

record was 600.60 mph, a mark that he held for the next five years.

His life then took a turn. Trans-Am racing was at its height and Craig became the American Motors Trans-Am car builder and racer. He took an AMX and proceeded to break Class B and C endurance

Chapter 3

Andy Brizio

It's a sign of great respect and admiration when an Italian family's patriarch is graced with the title of the Godfather. So it was in the California hot rod community as Andy Brizio's fame, popularity and reputation grew to the point where he was named "The Rodfather."

His credentials are undeniable, and include his having created the first street rod kit, having built the famed "Andy's Instant T" and having been an Oakland Roadster Show winner (1970). He has also served as the patriarch of one of hot rodding's great families, and has earned universal respect for his contributions to the sport.

The rewarding and productive career he forged was a departure from the bare-bones lifestyle into which he was born in the midst of the Depression.

Andy Brizio was born in 1932 to an Italian family in San Francisco's Mission District. It's ironic that his arrival coincided with the introduction of the famous 1932 Ford, which, like Andy, would turn out to be a hit with the hot rod community.

He led a typical Cal-kid lifestyle, graduating from Balboa High School just about the time the 1948 Ford was rolling off the line at the Ford Rouge River plant. During his high school years, he worked hard at getting a few extra dollars together so he could have his own wheels. Gas was cheap but good cars were hard to find, so Andy took to fixing them himself. He also became a milkman, but the cream for him was not on the top of the milk, it was his 1941 Plymouth and 1931 three-window coupe.

Hot rodding and drag racing in the early-fifties had a rather sour social stigma. "Those crazy kids out racing about in their hot rods," was the public view of what Andy Brizio was about to make his life's work. Growing up in San Francisco meant Andy met many people who were also involved with cars, and one such devotee was Jim McLennan. From McLen-

nan, who became the owner of three drag strips, including the famous Half Moon Bay track, Andy got the job as "official starter" at all three tracks.

Working as a starter at Half Moon Bay until its closing in the sixties, Andy got to know all the great cars and drivers. He flagged off Ivo and Garlits

It's the Oakland show in 1970, and Andy applies some elbow grease to put a show polish on the Instant T that won the show's top prize. His son Roy (foreground) makes sure dad doesn't miss a spot. A. Southard

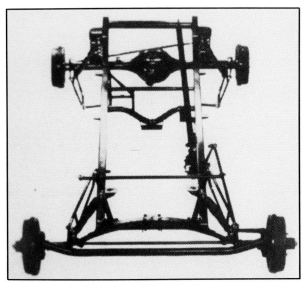

The original chassis for Andy's "Instant T" was plain and simple.

many times, and generally had a great time as a starter. This access to the world of speed led him into a life of fast cars as he also worked with McLennan in the famous Champion Speed Shop in South San Francisco.

During the fifties, Andy had also been married, had five children and gotten divorced. He set new directions in his life and, in 1960, he met the most influential person to enter his life, a woman named Sue Coontz. She had energy to match his and they married in 1963. Sue and Andy worked their separate ventures together, you might say; Andy worked the dragsters on the strip while Sue sold T-shirts, patches and decals out of the back of their station wagon in the pits.

From the age of three, Andy's son Roy hung out at his dad's side, always wide-eyed and asking questions, a habit that brought him the knowledge that made him the Rodfather's son, "the Rodmaster." Roy is the driving force behind Roy Brizio Street Rods in South San Francisco and is considered one of

A closer look at the Instant T, C-Cab Truck shows its gorgeous chrome running boards, lanterns mounted off the sides, luxuriously upholstered interior and the blown Chevy motor that was rich with chrome.

If you were looking for Andy in the early-sixties, it's a good bet you would find him at the starting line of the Half Moon Drags, where he was a legendary starter. He's flagging a drag here between two low-slung competitors.

A slightly elevated view of the Instant T Volksrod shows the VW engine in the rear, flanked by meaty tires. The interior is immaculate, with a wood-paneled dash, tight upholstery and a flashy chrome steering column. A. Southard

the world's foremost rod builders. His stunning Ferrari-powered 1932 took first place in the Oakland Roadster Show in 1987, which makes the Brizios the only father and son to each win hot rodding's most coveted trophy with their own cars.

In the early-sixties, Andy wanted to run his own business, and it was going to deal with hot rods, he was certain.

His ultra-modern hot rod shop, "Andy's," was on Mission Street in South San Francisco, right next door to Champion Speed Shop. It became *the* hang-out for the hot rod crowd. In this two-story building, Andy opened his parts shop upstairs; his warehouse and workshop were on the ground floor. Jim Nelson of Dragmaster supplied him with a T chassis, Andy pulled a body in from an Eastern supplier and scrounged up the other parts he needed. He went to all the swap meets, searching for T windshield posts and cowl lamps, as no one then made reproductions of them.

Andy sold some chassis kits using the Dragmaster frame but then decided he could build his own. His design was fabricated by Pete Odgen in Alamo, a small town just east of San Francisco, which is still the hub of fine car building and home to more than one famous rodder. Odgen made a jig and became Andy's "main man" in the chassis business. The Instant T idea was coming together.

Andy then built a complete car for a customer in Washington State for the seemingly immense sum of $5,000. Remember, this was 1967. After building a couple more complete cars, he stuck with his original

idea: to supply parts only, so a buyer could build his own rod. The Instant T became a reality. Andy's Instant T became a hot rodder's household word. Andy could supply a custom T chassis for $595. This included a complete dropped-axle front end, brakes, master cylinder, rear axle with gears, steering set-up and battery box.

Sue went on "search and buy" missions to swap meets in the East, to find enough windshield posts and cowl lamps to supply the growing market. She shipped them back to the shop, and Andy restored or repaired them before having them chrome-plated. Andy was also running a tire and wheel business as part of Instant T.

Sue went to work for American Racing Equipment, where she was the only woman in an office full of men. By working there she got to know many of the industry's leaders. John Buttera, hot rodding's greatest fabricator, became a close friend after coming to terms with "a woman who knew her wheels from her sewing box."

As the T business developed, so did Andy's rod-building ability. His first Instant T developed into the classic T Bucket. It featured a blown small-block engine with a chromed front end, four cowl lights and a white interior.

Not one to sit still for too long, Andy then put his energy into the first VW-powered street rod kit. The VW kit used a T roadster pickup body and a special tube chassis. It ran a dropped front axle and mated the VW motor and transaxle to the tube frame in its usual position. It was a practical, yet cute design, but

Here's a three-quarter rear view of the Instant T Volksrod. Andy's unique creation ran a dropped front axle and mated the VW motor and transaxle to the tube frame in its *usual position. The design was appealing and it worked well, but it had its doubters, apparently, because it never took off. Only around ten units were sold. A. Southard*

like many totally new and innovative products, it met with little success, selling only ten or so units.

The hot rod parts business continued to flourish, and the popularity of the Instant T had grown, too. The kit was now complete. For $738, customers got a body by A&I, a full chassis, a complete front end, a complete rear end, gears, a pedal cluster, a master cylinder, brakes, headlight brackets, shocks, springs, windshield posts and a battery box. His ads ran in several national magazines and Andy's Instant T made the name Brizio one to watch for.

In 1967, he drove his "Instant Volks T" to Gatlinburg, Tennessee, when rods weren't driven across country very much. It became one of the first East-meets-West hot rod adventures which are now commonplace in the hot rod community every summer. It was also the beginning of more than twenty cross-country hot rod trips that Andy would make in the next twenty years.

He built several famous rods besides his Ts, including the Golden Deuce and the C-Cab. (The C-Cab was eventually sold to the late John Bonham of the rock and roll group Led Zeppelin.) Andy won many trophies for his cars, but he wanted to win the biggie: Oakland.

The car that fulfilled this dream was his first Instant T, which went through three generations of development before it managed to stop the judges at the Oakland Roadster Show. It was purple, then red and black before it finally won "Most Beautiful Roadster" after Andy rebuilt it and had a wild paint job applied by Art and Ellen Himsl of Concord, California. Andy's T with its wild graphic paint scheme was the start of the graphics generation that today has turned into "usual business" for high-tech automotive finishes.

Andy tired of the constant demands that the rod business placed on him. He also had the tire and wheel business and an interest in Champion Speed Shop, which kept him busy, so in 1975, he handed the rod business over to his son Roy and continued to pursue his other interests.

An interior view of the Instant T shows that it was clean and simple. The attention to detail in Andy's cars was striking. A. Southard

After returning from the Peoria Street Rod Nationals one year, Andy ran this ad in Rod and Custom. It was indicative of his friendly nature and his growing national popularity and fame. His logo, which shows him cruising in a car loaded with parts, is appropriate since he was among the first to cross the nation in pursuit of valuable parts for his customs.

Another part of Andy's life that brought him to international rodding attention, of course, is his famous Andy's Picnic. Like many great events, it started out small, with just a few friends going on a mystery rod run. Twenty cars appeared at the

Andy, circa 1990, the successful owner of Andy's Tees, one of the West Coast's largest shirt-printing companies.

appointed time and drove up to Morton Hot Springs in the lower end of Sonoma county. There, Andy and Sue handed out free hot dogs and beer.

The reputation and location of the event changed several times over the years until the event became so big that the Vallejo Fairground was chosen to be its permanent home. The days of free hot dogs and beer are over. In the final year of free food and drinks, Andy handed out 7,000 hot dogs and 10,000 glasses of beer. Sue and Andy decided that they would have to handle the event differently, and now it is open to the public.

The essential non-competitive spirit of the event continues to draw a solid crowd and in its twenty-first anniversary, more than 1,600 hot rods rolled in. At each picnic, Andy cruises around to see old friends while hiding behind dark sunglasses and wearing his latest T-shirt. The picnic has now become *the* event to attend and many rodders from as far away as the East Coast have made it part of their summer schedule.

In 1980, Sue decided they should go back into the T-shirt business. They had sold their T-shirt company in the sixties to Dick Williams of Polyform fame. Sue and Andy visited a silk-screening show at the invitation of an old friend, Terry Cook, and what they saw fascinated and attracted them. Today, Andy and Sue have a successful custom T-shirt business based in Concord, California, selling under the name of "Andy's Tee Shirts."

To set up their T-shirt business, Andy and Sue sold their beloved hot rods. Suddenly, the Rodfather was without a rod. Roy decided that simply would not do, so he started work on a chassis. Nearing the job's completion, he discussed the project with an old family friend, Dennis Varney, who decided that it was time to call in a few favors. After all, the Rodfather had directly or indirectly helped many of the great names in the world of hot rodding and performance cars get their start.

Between Boyd Coddington, Buttera, Pete and Jake, Kenny Foster, Jack Williams, Magoo, Cub Barnett, Steve Archer, Jim Vickery and many others, Roy's custom-built chassis soon became the stunning 1932 that would make the Rodfather fully wheeled again. The plum-colored roadster was given to Andy as a surprise, just a few weeks before the 1990 Picnic, from a very appreciative son and group of friends.

With Sue and daughter Terri running the front office, Andy is still the man at the helm, taking care of the production side. Andy said that he has never worked harder in his life. His work schedule is usually twelve to fourteen hours a day, six days a week.

Since his early days as a man with a full head of hair and a beard, Andy's life has continued to run a hectic pace. The hair may be thinner and there may be an extra pound here and there, but Andy is still Andy Brizio, "the Rodfather," that tall, pleasant guy who brought us the world's first street rod kit.

Chapter 4

Art Chrisman

Art Chrisman was destined to succeed in the speed business. How could he fail? After all, he was ahead of the competition all along, or at least it seemed that way since he was spinning wrenches and working a torch when most other youngsters were still in short pants.

Born in Sulphur Springs, Arkansas, Art's family's life was automobiles. His father ran a successful auto

The Salt Flats were the place to be. That's Art at the right end of this group, wearing his 200 MPH Club T-shirt and holding a plaque he won. Note the tape across the open- *ings where the suspension exits the car's body. The openings were made as smooth as possible to cut wind drag.*

repair shop and did service work on farm machinery in the area. When the nation went to war in the forties, the Chrisman family went to California, where Art's father worked as a welder at the Todd Shipyards in San Pedro. While his father helped build Liberty ships, Art and his brother Lloyd were attending Compton Jr. High School and getting an introduction to the California world of hot rods.

At sixteen, Art owned a custom 1936 Ford sedan and was a member of the Saints Hot Rod Club. Having a father with a strong mechanical bent and talent as a fabricator would become instrumental in development of Art's interests.

The Chrisman and Sons Garage opened for business in Compton soon after World War II ended. The business flourished, offering a full range of automotive services, from transmission work to body and paint.

Both sons were active participants in local street racing and dry lakes activities. They built a number of race cars for the lakes, including a 1936 Ford four-door sedan. The car was used extensively for both the lakes and street racing, building its reputation as a hot machine as it hit 109 mph on the lakes and 90 mph at the Santa Ana Drags. Art still has the first prize from that event: a four-inch-high trophy.

Racing was a family affair, with Mom and Dad going along to oversee the day's activities (Mom with the fried chicken and Dad looking after the cars). Drag racing was magnetic for the boys, and they bought a three-window 1934 coupe and fitted it with a modified flathead. It was soon running 140 mph on the lakes.

Their talent for going fast was noted by many. In 1952, Art was working with Chet Herbert on a Tucker-powered streamliner, but a few weeks before Bonneville Speed Week, they destroyed the engine on the dyno. They quickly changed course and installed one of the new Chrysler Hemi engines and hauled the streamliner out to the Salt Flats.

On the Salt Flats, they were plagued by numerous engine and weather problems. On the last day of racing, the nitro- and alcohol-powered streamliner was running like a song—but their driver deserted the team. Art was immediately shifted from team wrench to driver, which proved to be a great move. Art's two-way average was 235 mph, a new class record. It also gave him instant membership in the 200 MPH Club.

1953 proved to be a memorable year for the Chrismans. They showed a style and class for hot rodding that is still a landmark today. They started

The Chrisman family's 1934 Ford ran 140 mph on the dry lakes in 1950.

Turn back the clock to 1956 and here's the coupe waiting for a push-off on the Bonneville Salt Flats. The sleek car ran 196 mph.

After a dramatic, last-minute move to the cockpit, Art drove the Chet Herbert streamliner to a two-run average speed of 235 mph in 1952. He was a mechanic for the Hemi-powered car until the last minute, when the original driver decided he didn't want to pilot it across the Salt Flats. Art took over and immediately joined the 200 MPH Club.

Hustler I, dressed in its new aluminum skin, rolls off the line at the Santa Ana Drags.

building the famous Chrisman '30 coupe. It was to be a salt and lakes car. Initially, it was run in Class C, powered by a flathead, but this was soon changed to an Ardun conversion.

In 1954, it took both Class C and B records at 180 mph. A transformation for 1955 converted it to a 331-ci Hemi running on fuel injection and alcohol. In

Class D, it again took the record with 190 mph and upped it further to 196 mph. During one attempt, Art spun through the traps, running 189 mph, and still managed to qualify for the record run.

By this stage, the coupe had been extensively modified into its perfect salt and lakes look. Setting it on a custom-built tube frame, they chopped the top about twelve inches, channeled it and sectioned the body. Eventually, the Chrisman coupe was sold and in 1957, George Barris picked it up and converted it for the "Dobie Gillis Show" on TV.

The coupe eventually resurfaced in the hands of Bob Larrivie, Sr., the promoter of the ISCA (International Show Car Association) show car circuit, and came back into Art's life. Larrivie wanted the coupe restored and Art was the obvious person to do it justice. Art and his son restored the coupe to ten-point condition and it was later featured again in *Hot Rod* magazine in a full-color spread.

Running alongside the Chrisman coupe was another famous hot rod which would go down in the history books of hot rodding, the Chrisman Track T roadster. Purchased in 1953, it had seen action as a sprint car and street hot rod in the hands of LeeRoy Neumeyer.

The Chrisman boys had seen Neumeyer's Track T roadster about the Santa Ana area for years and finally, in 1953, they managed to snag it. The Track T

"Hustler I" was a tire-smoking, 180-mph, top fuel dragster Art and the clan built to tear up the tracks.

has also been part of another hot rodder's life; a young Wally Parks had wrenched on it in the thirties.

It became their drag racer and went through extensive modification, including stretching. They were entrants at the National Hot Rod Association's (NHRA) first National in Great Bend, Indiana. Running against the San Diego "Bean Bandits," Art managed a blazing 149–mph run before the rains washed the event out and before he could rebuild the self-destructing transmission.

When the event was rescheduled for Phoenix, Arizona, Art was up against Calvin Rice in his Chrysler-powered rail. The Track T was powered by a series of flathead engines. It also competed on the sand at Daytona Speed Week with Bill Stroppe wrenching the Ford.

The Chrismans stayed on the pace with the others in the sport, adding a new partner, Frank Cannon, and forming the team of Chrisman & Cannon. They built "Hustler I," a blown, Thunderbird-powered fuel dragster. At first, it used a Potvin crank-driven GMC blower turning 160 mph, but that soon changed to a 450–ci injected gas Hemi which moved the speed scale up into the 180–mph zone with 8.20 ETs. Hustler I took the team to many southern California track records.

Art had many ideas, including building a dual Hemi-engined dragster. It used a twin pair of rear wheels set apart so that one engine drove the inner set of wheels and a second engine drove the outer wheels. Art could not get the correct weight transfer he sought and abandoned the project after six months of testing. In 1959, he introduced his sidewinder-style, rear-engined dragster. It got the better of him, though, when the engine collapsed and struck him from behind, causing extensive injuries during a run; but within six months, Art was back at the wheel.

The Chrisman family business grew into a six-stall garage with plenty of customer work flowing through the doors, and work on the race cars took up the rest of the family's time.

In 1957, Art took the T to Daytona Beach for Speed Week. It was powered by a Stroppe-prepared 312–ci Mercury ohv engine. Art also drove the Stroppe-prepared, modified Mercury convertible, with a streamlined nose and vertical stabilizer, on the beach. He logged a record speed of 159 mph.

Through his contacts and experience with the drag racing and high performance crowd, Art eventually was offered a job as the western technical representative for Autolite Spark Plugs in 1962. He attended Indy, Pikes Peak, the drag race circuit, the boat drags and the speedway for the next ten years on behalf of the spark plug manufacturer.

Through his job with Autolite, Art worked with Mickey Thompson on his funny cars in the early-seventies and with Mario Andretti on his four-cam Indy-engined car, which helped him qualify at 200 mph. He also oversaw Autolite's dyno facility at Signal Hill in Long Beach, which offered racers a chance to use the dyno for engine development work.

Other members of the Chrisman family were drag racing. Jack Chrisman, Art's uncle, was the driver of the Sachs & Sons AF/X Mercury Comet and later the Kendall GT-1 Mercury Comet Funny Car.

In 1973, Art started running a dyno facility for Ed Pink in Garden Grove, California. This work included a six-year contract with W & R Grace and TRW pistons. Other testing included ignition parts and wheels, as well as vehicle and emissions certification. It developed into a facility that SEMA (Specialty Equipment Manufacturers Association) used for testing, and later became a test station for grey market import vehicles to obtain federal smog emission certification.

In the early eighties, Art again opened his own shop, this time in Anaheim, California, to specialize in restorations. His first project was a ten-point 1965 Shelby GT restoration. In its first time out, it won

Art's six-wheeled, two-engined dragster suffered from severe weight-transfer problems and was eventually scrapped.

Art the Autolite man inspects the plugs of Mickey Thompson's Ford funny car.

Art Chrisman, circa 1990, sporting a "Hustler I" T-shirt.

first place. Next, his old Bonneville coupe was returned to him after Bob Larrivie had purchased it from George Barris.

It took some convincing on Larrivie's part to get Art to do the restoration but who better to restore the car? It, too, was a ten-point restoration, which was featured once again in a color spread in *Hot Rod* magazine as the classic Bonneville coupe of all time.

Since that restoration, Art moved to another facility in Santa Ana, California, and opened a new shop under the name of "CARS." Here, he maintains his collection of Hustler dragsters which he still races at nostalgia drag racing events all over the country.

Art Chrisman has slowed his pace a little, but he continues to build some of hot rodding's most intriguing vehicles, including a Corvette-powered Jaguar XJ-S and a string of new roadsters.

Chapter 5

Bill Cushenberry

Bill Cushenberry might just be proof that not all prodigies are born, some are made.

As a lad in Wichita, Kansas, where he lived for twenty-five years after being born in Alabama in 1933, Bill got early hands-on experience with automotive work. After classes at Wichita's North High, Bill spent his free time at the shop of his Uncle Max, whom Bill described as one of those people who "could take anything apart and put it back together again."

Bill picked up that same trait, but had a knack for customizing things before he put them back together. He got his first chance to jazz up an otherwise stock car when he bought his first ride, a 1940 Plymouth.

At sixteen, Bill rented a stall in an old, two-pump gas station on the northeast side of Wichita. He hammered fenders and wrenched on cars. His first professional custom work came from this business. He had taught himself to "lead" after watching a few older body men ply their trade in body repair shops in the local neighborhood. He bought himself the raw supplies and a lead paddle, and it didn't take him long to get a handle on tinning the surface. He soon had the process perfected.

The Car Craft *"Dream Rod"* that Bill fashioned featured gold pearl paint and a fully dressed Ford 289.

Bill posed at the Los Angeles Hot Rod Show with the Matador, a car built from a 1940 Ford coupe.

His first full-custom used a 1949 two-door Ford sedan. Then came a 1948 Frazer with dual headlights, faded fenders and molded drip rails. His repair shop flourished, but it wasn't what Bill enjoyed most.

The "California Custom Look" was in, and Hollywood still had a magic ring to its name. The new *Hop Up* and *Hot Rod* magazines had made their way East, and their influence was strongly felt among the rodders and customizers of the time. Bill remembers reading the magazines, absorbing every

The interior view of the Matador shows its rimless steering wheel. The car was almost like a collection of Bill's greatest customizing hits, with its chopped roof, sectioned body and incredible styling touches every inch of the way.

page with glee. Over the next five years, he continued to develop his custom techniques, shaving hoods and handles, chopping tops and frenching headlights.

Drag racing had become a high-line interest among the hot rod crowd thanks to the influence of *Hot Rod* magazine and the sport's unique and inexpensive racing ideas. Bill was one of the participants at the first NHRA National held at the airport in Great Bend, Indiana, in 1955. He had built the Lyle Fisher Speed Sport A/Open Gas 1927 T slingshot, which was powered by a Hemi. The dragster was called "Sneaky Beaky." Bill had fabricated the nose out of a pair of Hudson fenders, hence the name.

In 1957, Bill married and opened the Kansas Custom Shop, where he built his famous 1957 Oldsmobile Holiday coupe for Bill Moore. But the lure of California, with its flowering racing and customizing scenes, were too great an attraction for "a kid from Kansas," and in 1958, Bill moved to Monterey. Bill had pre-arranged a job with Butts Cadillac through a family friend, and it was waiting for him when he arrived. He worked in the body and paint section for a year before opening his own part-time shop at 2400 Del Monte in Monterey.

He joined the Slow Pokes Car Club and as his reputation for quality work spread, his part-time body and customizing business quickly began to grow. His customers came from San Francisco and Los Angeles, as well as the local scene. By the end of 1959, Bill had resigned from Butts Cadillac to run his own shop full time, continuing body work by day and custom work by night.

His shop became a central Californian mecca for customs. Bill built Tony Cardoza's 1959 Impala and the famous "Matador" 1940 Ford coupe. The Matador featured a perfect combination of custom tricks for its restyling. Bill chopped two inches off the roof, three inches from the posts, and the body was sectioned four-and-one-half inches. Added to this major surgery were other styling ideas that would take the Matador to the top of the class with a long list of show wins, including the Bakersfield Autorama, where Bill collected a twelve-foot-high trophy. (The Matador was later sold to Bob Larrivie in Detroit for $4,000 in 1963.)

Bill's reputation as an automotive artist spread across the country. Ford commissioned him to build a custom 1962 Galaxie 500 427 convertible for the traveling Ford Custom Car Caravan. Bill enjoyed working on the project, but it took him out of the workshop for months at a time, traveling with both the "Silhouette" and the "Astro" to show them on behalf of Ford. The Astro featured double-round, frenched headlights, French Pearl Blue paint and a white pearl Naugahyde interior by Bill Manger of Castroville.

With the Ford project completed, Bill decided to move operations to Burbank, where he shared

Bill posed with the Matador, a flowing, sculpted beauty.

The Tony Cardoza 1959 Impala custom featured a full-custom O-front, a Candy Apple Red paint job and chrome-reversed rims.

As evidenced by this stretched-out beauty, Bill's talents as a builder included the ability to chop, channel and do sectioned modifications as well as doing molded body work and custom paint.

space with Lee Wells Upholstery. There, he did free-lance work for George Barris, refashioning the Ford Futura show car into the "Batmobile."

Hot on the heels of the Matador project came Bill's first complete, one-off hot rod custom. Illustra-tor Don Varner and Bill became close friends and concocted a wild custom street rod they called the Silhouette. It was built on a modified 1956 Buick chassis and featured a hand-formed steel body.

At the NHRA "Big Show West" Winternationals hot rod and custom show, Bill collected "Grand Sweepstakes Custom" for the Silhouette. (The Sil-houette is still available as a model kit.)

Bill continued to work on customers' cars but fortunately this "bread and butter work" did not get in the way of his next project: the *Car Craft* "Dream Rod."

Commissioned by Bob Larrivie, its asymmetri-cal lines were an instant hit. The Dream Rod was built on a sixty-eight-inch Jowett Jupiter chassis using tubular frame sub-structures and a VW front suspension. The rod featured radio-controlled doors, trunk, starter and lights. The interior was fully cus-tomized with the imaginative use of a Mercury instrument panel mounted on the head of the con-sole, and pearl Naugahyde upholstery.

The body followed Cushenberry's traditional use of all steel. Using a Pontiac cowl, Studebaker windscreen and parts of a 1960 Corvair, Bill fash-ioned the remainder of the body by hand. The body

The "Astro" was a custom Ford 427–powered Galaxie 500 built for the Ford Custom Car Caravan in 1962. It had double-round frenched headlights and a gorgeous French Pearl Blue interior.

On the set of the television program, "The Wonderful World of Wheels," the Silhouette was in the spotlight.

was finished in a special Cushenberry Gold Pearl tint called Desert Sand. Powering the rod was a fully decorated Ford 289. At the time, the Dream Rod was valued at $15,000.

Customs were fading from the scene. Super Stock drag racing was just starting to make the big time and the man in the street was "changing gears" towards muscle cars. Bill worked on a number of projects with Dean Jeffries, then moved into the classic car restoration business.

In his shop in Burbank, Bill restored a number of Dual Ghias, including one for Frank Sinatra. Next, a Bugatti project took about two years of solid work, but it was not the type of restoration that Bill wanted to do. He preferred later-model vehicles and specialized in Mercedes 300SL roadsters and Gullwings.

Bill began to tire of the fast-paced lifestyle in Los Angeles: too much work and too much traffic. The boy from the Midwest wanted to see a little more open country around him, so in 1974 he moved north to Bakersfield, California, where he opened

Bill Cushenberry, Bakersfield, California, 1990.

another shop to do custom work on Porsche 911s and 914s and restoration work on Mercedes 300s.

In the early-nineties, Bill is still open for business in Bakersfield, where he continues to work on Mercedes Gullwing restorations. Just like the old days, his skill with sheet metal work continues in his tradition of perfect metal craftsmanship.

Chapter 6

Jim Deist

Take a thousand people at any racetrack and you'll find that 999 of them are concerned with how fast they can make their cars go. For years, though, drivers across the country have been thanking their lucky stars that the thousandth guy at the track was a man like Jim Deist, someone who was vitally interested in seeing how he could slow cars down and keep their drivers safe after they've built up all that great speed.

Combining common sense, an acute awareness of the principles of motion and a study of safety materials' reliability, Jim has crafted a full assortment of safety products to keep generations of performance drivers and full-on racers safe and sound.

Whether at the dry lakes or Bonneville, on the road circuits of the SCCA (Sports Car Club of America) or the banked ovals of NASCAR (National Association for Stock Car Automobile Racing), the Deist logo has graced safety equipment and brought reassurance to go-fast drivers for more than four decades.

Jim grew up as a second-generation German-American lad in Glendale, California, and he had an open-eyed interest in mechanics and sciences. After classes at Hoover High School, he learned about the cars of the day while pumping gas and tinkering at his father's service station.

He liked automobiles and worked on them whenever possible. First, he bought a 1928 Ford

Jim Deist inspected an early ribbon chute in his shop.

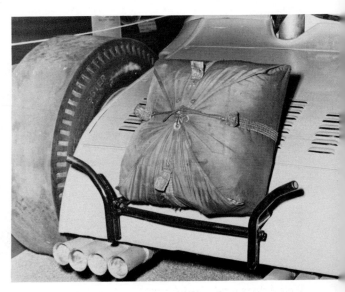

One of Deist's early sixteen-foot ribbon chutes was mounted on the 1960 Speed Sport drag racer.

A collector's item: An early Deist decal from the sixties. Note that area codes and prefixes weren't spelled out in telephone numbers at the time.

The helmet for an early Deist funny car fire suit was not streamlined, but it was safe and effective, which was the goal, after all.

sedan, but quickly replaced it with a T roadster. He became involved with the dry lakes racing crowd, running a Model B Ford on Rosemond. He modified the roadster to a lakes roadster with a V–8 60 and a log manifold, and drove it out to the lakes early on a Saturday morning for testing.

During the car's first run, the flywheel came loose, damaging the bolts. A late-afternoon trip to the last parts shop open in Lancaster let Jim get the roadster back together for the clock on Sunday. Sunday's run had the roadster through the traps at 120 mph, but he dropped a rod—and had to build a

new motor. Street racing was also one of his part-time sports, and Jim remembers many hot runs on Friday nights in the San Fernando Valley.

After the war, he worked at various jobs, not finding anything in particular that he wanted to do

Walt Arfons used Deist chutes for his Green Monster jet car, which was basically a jet engine mounted on wheels with a fearless driver perched up front.

professionally. He married Marian Hoving in 1947 and continued tooling about with the hot rod crowd.

He took a job with Irving Air Chute, a manufacturer of aircraft braking, cargo and military refueler parachutes. There, he found a niche as an engineering assistant, which fulfilled his interest in mechanics

Considering that it was the true pioneering era in safety suit construction and materials, this early Deist top fuel fire suit was actually quite well-fitted. It featured the lobster tail seat, which expanded as the driver sat or crouched.

and the sciences. Not a man of traditional academic training, Jim attended night school so he could better understand his work.

One morning, he received a call from a friend at Lockheed whose son, a drag racer, was having trouble stopping his Plymouth race car. He asked Jim if he could make his son a braking parachute for the Plymouth. The son had very little cash, but Jim decided that the idea was sound and promised to help out when he could find an old chute.

Jim found an old Air Force ribbon parachute that had been discarded as unrepairable. He spent four hours "Mickey Mousing" the chute together for the Plymouth, and it worked well.

In 1956, Bob Berssett asked Jim if he could get him a chute for his 104-mph slingshot dragster. Jim made a chute, packed with a mounting board and a release. The first time out, it fouled around the T push bar on the back of the dragster, but a piece of cardboard and some tape temporarily corrected the problem. The crowd at Lions Drag Strip saw a demonstration of Jim's parachute on his 1954 Lincoln. It was here that the racers saw the great potential of the chute. Art Chrisman was the next to coax Jim into a new chute for his "Hustler."

By this time, Jim had risen within Irving to become a project engineer and was developing many missile recovery and aircraft parachutes for the Air Force. The work was exciting and highly confidential. He worked on drop-test vehicles, anti-spin parachutes and braking chutes for the A4-D attack fighter and other classified Air Force and aerospace projects.

Jim's personal interest in fast cars continued. He saw new market potential with drag chutes for Irving, and approached the company with his idea. He was turned down flat. They didn't want to be involved with a bunch of hot rodders. After ten years with Irving Air Chute, Jim decided to change course. Even though he was project manager of the seat belt testing lab, when Irving moved from Glendale to Gardena, Deist resigned.

His ideas had caught the attention of many car racers, including Mickey Thompson, who was about to restart the age of the Land Speed Records. The Thompson "Challenger" soon became a Deist project. Jim liked the drag racing at speed trials because instead of standing around for five hours waiting for the Air Force to run a single test, he could spend a few hours at a drag site and come home with the results of a dozen or more tests.

Jack Chrisman bought a chute from Deist for his famous 180-mph Hustler dragster. Chrisman found it not only helped him stop but made him a better crowd draw at events. "Come and see the man who goes so fast, he has to stop his car with a parachute," squalled the radio ads.

For Jim, 1958 was "the year of change." He set up shop at home with just enough equipment to start making his own products. He had several sewing machines and a nylon tacker, and being a handyman, he also built a simple nylon cutter. He installed these in his garage, where he and Marian cut and assembled parachutes and safety belts.

"Deist" became the first name in safety. Many of the day's racers came to Jim for seatbelts, chutes and other simple safety items. The Arfons, Craig Breedlove and Gary Gabliech all sought custom equipment from him. For the Land Speed Record racers, Jim devised a tube pack with a conical spring to eject a chute into the air flow behind the car.

Jim had seen some disastrous fuel fires at the drag strip and tossed a few driver protection ideas around in his head for quite some time. He was aware of all the details of Air Force fire safety clothing, but none suited the drag racer. The concept finally came together as a head-to-toe suit. Jim felt he could design a suit that would give a driver good heat radiation protection for up to one minute.

His first suit was made of aluminized cotton with a foam Traco lining. It was hand-sewn by Jim's mother. The suit was tailored for Tommy Dryer, who was soon nicknamed "The Tin Man."

He raced in it for twelve months and never needed its protection. Then struck the very reason that Dryer was wearing it: an engine fire fried his car.

Jim recalled being told by the fire marshalls at the track, "Boy, there is no way that this guy is going to get out of this wreck alive." But Dryer emerged virtually unscathed. The suit had protected him just as Jim had designed it to do. Dryer was also wearing one of Jim's seatbelts, which had been installed only two weeks earlier.

There were problems with the suit and the way it fit, however. Jim designed a new "lobster tail" for the seat of the suit. This gave it a section in the seat of the pants that would bend and fold to better conform to the driver's crouched seating position. More detailing followed, with lobster tail knees and elbow pads, and so did more orders.

Business was prospering and Jim opened a separate speed shop. There he sold a range of performance items, as well as his own products. This section of the business was later sold to a partnership that included Art Linkletter.

Other parts of the business were also growing. Jim was making ejection seat harnesses for the Air Force and designing and fabricating survival equipment packs and parachutes for NASA to use on the Apollo moon missions. Other people sought his help: For the movie industry, Jim made safety harnesses for stuntmen, and for the Los Angeles Police S.W.A.T. team, he made a special vest.

The original ribbon chute design gave way to this, the ring chute style.

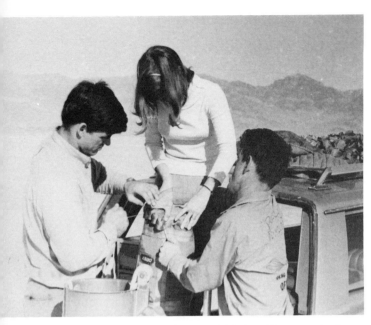

The Deist crew packs one of Mickey Thompson's chutes before a run in May 1970.

The high speeds of the late-sixties prompted the National Hot Rod Association (NHRA) to make parachutes mandatory on cars running faster than 150 mph, which dramatically increased the demand for Jim's parachutes.

This motivated Jim to design a new series of parachutes. Ribbon chutes had been fine in the early years, but they were expensive. They also required considerable time to manufacture and were very susceptible to damage. Next followed ring chutes, which were made with concentric, circular rings of fabric. These became the standard for a number of years. Eventually, they were replaced by square parachutes and, later, by cross parachutes.

The personal clothing lines also developed. The invention by DuPont of Nomex expanded the styles and possible constructions of fireproof suits. Deist now offers several different layer combinations, as well as a larger variety of suit styles for any form of motorsport, from Formula 1 to Top Fuel suits.

Deist Safety has grown into one of the leading racing safety equipment companies in the world. Jim has a research and development lab next to his office. He is a regular at Bonneville, ever helpful with items related to safety. He also owns the "American Challenge," a jet "World Water Speed" boat powered by a J46 jet from an F&U Cutlass fighter.

Jim is a complex man who is forever taking on new projects. His interest has always included not only how fast his clients go, but how to safely get them back to zero without a scratch, no matter what the racing conditions. Racers appreciate what personal protection means, and many of them proudly wear fireproof clothing with a small, black, oval-shaped logo on the arm that simply reads, "Deist."

As the Deist chute operation developed, it began to produce customized chutes with advertising and logos like this one for a Ford racer.

Chapter 7

Bill Devin

California has long been the state where concepts and inventive thoughts are converted from dreams into reality. For decades, Americans who wanted the chance to start anew, think freely and spread their wings have migrated to the Golden State. Following World War II, the state underwent a dramatic period of growth, and since then it has been the birthplace of inventions as varied as the dune buggy and the

SS models were being produced on the assembly line at the El Monte factory. Louis Unser is at right, digging in his tool box.

personal computer. Even products or ideas that stem from other sources will likely get altered, modified or improved once they're in the hands of open-minded Californians.

Our interest here, of course, is unique performance automobiles, and one of the futurists who has come up with ideas before the rest of the world, Bill Devin. The list of Bill's original ideas and pursuits could rival those coming out of the giant automotive research centers. Some of his ideas have included: tooth-belt-drive overhead cams; a sports/race car with an 850-cc engine that could blow off a Jaguar 120 back in the fifties; the first four-barrel aluminum manifold for a small-block Chevy engine; the first real fiberglass production kit cars; and a perfected version of the VW kit car.

Bill Devin has been a quiet achiever all his life. He was born in Oklahoma, where his father owned the Chevrolet dealership in a town called Rocky. Oklahoma was still fighting off the shackles of the Depression when Bill's father decided that California held a brighter future for the family. In 1939, the family moved to the West Coast. Bill started work with the Douglas Aircraft Company and in 1942 joined the Navy.

He returned to California at the war's end and tried to open a new car dealership. Unsuccessful on his first attempt, he moved to Montour, Iowa, and tried again. Within two years, he had a Chrysler dealership and a number of farm machinery agencies. After building a new showroom the next year, he sold the dealership and moved back to California. His automotive ventures in California prospered as he owned several Chrysler dealerships in Fontana.

By this time, Bill was involved in racing, on a small scale, perhaps, but fast and competitively. He owned a Crosley Hot Shot powered by a 720-cc engine. Bill sought a faster car and soon hooked up with Luigi Chinetti and Ernie McAfee, who were working out a deal to import Siata and Ferrari sports cars into the United States.

Bill traveled to Europe, planning to race the twenty-four hours of Le Mans. He needed a car, so he ordered a three-liter Pininfarina coupe but, unfortunately, the Ferrari wasn't finished in time for the race. Bill wasted no time in Europe, however. He visited many small Italian custom body builders, absorbing a vast bank of background knowledge. He ordered four cars, including some of the most beautiful early Ferrari and Siata sports cars imported into this country.

One story Bill loves to tell about Ferrari took place in the early fifties. Like any small company, Ferrari was often short of cash, so when Bill turned

A Devin mechanic worked on one of Devin's front-wheel-drive Panhard racers.

A Devin D underwent testing at the old Riverside
Raceway.

A nearly-completed Devin SS body and chassis awaited
final assembly.

The SS was the ultimate Devin, with great speed, handling and braking for a car built in 1959. It could run from zero-to-sixty in 5.7 seconds with its Chevy V–8, and could go from zero-to-100 in 10 seconds flat.

up with a $10,000 banker's check to pay for the cars he wanted from Ferrari, the "Commadore" personally drove him to the bank to cash the check.

Bill returned to California ready to move in his own direction. He severed his ties with Chinetti and McAfee, sold his Ferrari and took cash and a French Deutsch-Bonnet sports car, or DB for short, in trade for the three-liter coupe. He also bought the French Panhard agency and in this deal obtained ten chassis and one body. Bill knew he had a hot little racer that just needed some development.

The 750–cc, twin-cylinder, horizontally opposed engine was very radical for the early-fifties, and for

The Devin D, with Bill behind the wheel. This car evolved from an idea Bill got in 1957, to build a two-seater on a VW platform. The car came complete, or as a kit. More than 300 were sold, even though Porsche and VW dealers were instructed not to cooperate with factory and consumers' attempts to buy engines for the D.

this engine, Bill created the first toothed-belt-drive overhead cam setup. Using Manx Norton racing motorcycle heads, he built a tensioned drive system. He designed a super-stiff, lightweight eighty-four-inch chassis, upon which he mounted the Panhard engine, front suspension with drive system and complete rear suspension. The body came from his DB. The little French car was not the best-looking beast ever built, but it was the right size, and was to be Bill's first fiberglass car. As he said, "I didn't know anything about fiberglass; I just did it."

The outcome was an interesting-looking little car, very aerodynamic and lightweight. The Devin-Panhard weighed 950 pounds, ready to race. There was such a great power-to-weight ratio that off the line, a Devin-Panhard could whip a Mercedes 190SL. "It will never work!" said John Bond of *Road & Track* fame about the ohc system. (Funny enough, though, it worked great!)

Other additions included a larger capacity, so that he could run in the next class up, and a Roots blower. The Pebble Beach Race in 1956 saw Bill clean up in his class and then top that by beating everything home, including the XK–120 Jaguars. Quite an achievement for a funny little car built by a "shade tree mechanic." In 1956, the Devin-Panhard became a 750–cc class champion. Another extraordinary coincidence was that three years later, Porsche patented an idea that was Bill's idea first: the tooth-drive-belt ohc.

Bill's success with the little racer prompted him to think about building a road-going sports car. The information gathered on his early-fifties trip to Europe gave Bill a unique perspective of construction techniques for building short-run sports cars. He had Murray Nichols design a new car. The first attempt was abandoned and the second attempt wound up in court, but Bill pressed on. He knew what he wanted and no one was going to stop him from building his dream sports car.

An Italian Ermini sports car came into his possession for a time. The Ermini resembled a Scaglietti-bodied Ferrari. It was cute and about the right dimensions for the one Bill envisioned. Using that body, Bill built a plug, extending and modifying the design to suit his concept. He fitted a dash and a cockpit liner that included the seats (a first for kit cars). This plug was used for a mold and from it several bodies were produced.

From this one car, Bill proceeded over the next few years to construct a huge variety of body variations with longer wheelbases and wider tracks in twenty-seven different combinations. Because of Bill's nature as a perfectionist, he made sure that his molding and glasswork were ripple-free and smooth.

Bill was now in the sports car market, able to offer a sports car of considerable sophistication with a tubular frame and independent I-beam front suspension. The rear used a narrowed axle, radius rods

44

and a transverse spring. It was powered by a V–8 and an owner's choice of gearbox. Business was brisk. A buyer could get a chassis and body kit for $995 or have Devin build the car.

An international inquiry gave Bill's project a shot in the arm. He flew to Belfast to meet an Irish sports car builder who wanted bodies for a super-fast, Jag-powered chassis he had designed and built. Bill was highly impressed with what he saw and on the spot ordered the chassis complete with fully independent suspension. The frame was tubular, three-inch mid-steel, crossed-braced and framed with two-inch steel tubing. The front suspension was revised with aluminum A-arms and special coil-over shocks by Woodhead-Monroe. It used tight two-and-one-half turns, lock-to-lock, rack-and-pinion steering. The rear suspension was a De Dion tube design with parallel trailing links and shocks. Brakes were to be twelve-inch Girlings discs at the front and eleven-inch inboard discs at the rear. The rear sus-pension was to be an independent design of Bill's, but that had to wait.

Its power came from a 283 Chevy V–8. Bill wanted to fit a single Holley four-barrel carburetor, but nobody made one, so Bill designed and built one. Like his cars, it could be ordered in a variety of ways: The manifold could be adapted to run a two- or four-barrel carburetor or even adapted to use a supercharger. As with so many of Bill's designs, it was years ahead of its time. The manifold was so successful that the Sprint Car Association banned its use. That in itself is an honor but is not conducive to good sales. Over the next few years, the Devin body was refined with a larger grille opening, a different line to the rear body work and in-fender fuel tanks.

The Devin was a flexible design. The body could be mated to many chassis. Several hybrids were spawned, including MG-Devins, Porsche-Devins and Crosley-Devins. But the primary effort was aimed at producing a super-fast Ferrari beater. Pete Woods became Class C champion in a Devin SS in 1959. Bill had given him the responsibility of promoting and marketing the SS through Evans Industries. The SS, which was the ultimate Devin, was a high-speed car. It did all the right things. Not only was it blindingly quick for 1959, it also handled and stopped with great aplomb. Its zero-to-sixty time with a 220-hp Chevy V–8 was 5.7 seconds—fantastic then and certainly acceptable today. It could run the quarter mile in fourteen seconds and hit 100 mph in ten seconds flat.

Others were also having great success with the Devin. Ak Miller won the sports car class four years running at Pikes Peak in a Devin. The name "Devin"

The Devin C. The "C" in the name stood for Corvair, and the car was powered by a turbocharged Corvair flat six. It was shown at the 1962 New York Auto Show and was raced at the Pikes Peak Hillclimb later that year.

This cutaway shows off the Devin SS with its Chevy V-8 engine. It was the only front-engine Devin.

Devin's most famous roadster, Moonbeam, blasted down the Lions Dragstrip, smoking its tires. This photo was taken by hot rodding legend and talented photographer Dean Moon.

became well-known, and others in the automotive world were eyeing the Devin with intense interest.

Dean Moon, the speed equipment manufacturer from Santa Fe Springs, California, built "Moonbeam." It was to be a Devin like no other—a straight-line car, a speed-record quality car and a drag race special. Moonbeam was built on a one-hundred-inch wheelbase and fifty-four-inch track. Today, it is powered by a tri-pack Ford flathead V-8 cranked up with a heap of special Moon racing performance parts and other early speed equipment.

Moon built the car for promotions and testing. Its racing history includes traveling to the Old World, where it won the Brighton Speed Trials. To the delight of British spectators, it smoked off the line in a blaze of acceleration never before seen in Merry Old England. Moonbeam was also raced at Bonneville and El Mirage dry lake. At Bonneville in 1959, it topped the 200–mph mark, powered by a 645–hp blown Chevy small-block. The engine was fitted with a crank-driven Potvin blower, another of Moon's special performance items.

One of Bill Devin's greatest contributions was to the kit car industry midway through his years of producing Devin cars. In 1957, he proposed a two-seater on a shortened VW platform. His next project revolved around this idea: the Devin D. This car was available complete or as a kit, and was based on Porsche or VW running gear and chassis with a custom-made Devin body and frame. Bill sold more than 300 variations of the D, despite obstacles that included VW and Porsche instructing dealers not to sell new engines for Devin cars.

The next model out of the Devin works was the Model C in 1960. The C stood for Corvair. Andy Granatelli borrowed one, gave it a supercharger and turned a speed of 109 mph for the quarter and 167 mph at Bonneville, all in the same month. The C also acquitted itself exceptionally well in slalom racing.

By 1964, Bill had built two coupes for the New York Motor Show. Under great pressure from the major manufacturers, especially GM, Bill's display was put at the back of the show. Bill was giving the Corvette some strong competition on the race track, and Chevrolet wanted him well out of the limelight.

GM approached him for the specifications of his independent rear suspension, which he gladly supplied. However, when he called the research facility to ask whether he could do any development work for GM, the reply was, in effect, "What could *you* do for GM? We have thousands of designers."

John Bond, who had just visited the GM research facilities in 1959, met with Bill in southern California and John inquired if Bill was working for GM. John had seen a Devin at the GM development center, jacked up with the rear end hanging out! Such are the problems of not patenting your design work—something Bill never bothered to do for any of his innovative projects.

By the end of 1964, Bill had had enough and closed his operation. During the years, he had produced more than 3,380 Devins. He had designed a car that could thrash the Corvette of the times into the weeds. He had designed an overhead cam system that could really be called his own, and that today is used by every major automaker.

Devin cars always had style and horsepower and were consistent race winners, but most important of all, they were built by a man who could see where the automobile was going when most people still had their heads stuck in the "Stovebolt Six" age.

During the mid-sixties, Bill worked as a consultant to afterparts manufacturers and then began a successfull real estate career. Today, he is working again on his Devins. He is completing a number of his unfinished projects, including finishing the second GT coupe, restoring others and remanufacturing some of his older products.

Bill Devin is an amazing man of the auto industry, a maverick builder who through storms, successes and failures, maintained clever hands, a brain and a keen eye that could see the world beyond the end of the production line. He is one of few people who can say, "I have built my own car"—and a great one it is at that!

Chapter 8

Vic Edelbrock

If not for fate and its deliverance of a devastating fire upon a small Kansas grocery store, the automotive aftermarket might today be without one of its greatest names.

That name is Edelbrock, the same name on the sign at a Wichita grocery store in the twenties. The father of Vic Edelbrock, Sr., supported his family well with that store until it was wiped out by a fire one morning in 1927. Vic, who was just 15, had to quit school and find work to help his family survive.

He had a mechanical bent which he was able to nurture while working at auto repair shops. When the Depression hit, it hit Kansas hard, and Vic looked for opportunities like those that his brother was seeking in California. Vic and his wife moved west, join-

Vic is all smiles after his midget has again cleaned up on the competition at Ascot.

ing his brother on the coast. He found a job parking cars while his wife worked as a maid. It wasn't glamorous, but it was work, and it helped them make enough to get by in those tough times.

Vic saved enough money, in fact, to open his own car repair shop with a brother-in-law on Wilshire Boulevard in Beverly Hills. The repair business flourished and in 1934, he moved into his own shop on the corner of Venice and Hoover in Los Angeles. It was a small three-pump gas station with a one-stall garage.

Around this time, Vic became interested in building for speed. In his shop, he began experimenting with a 1931 Chrysler roadster. He rebuilt the roadster engine, body and frame, added a few modifications and used it as his daily driver. In 1937, he moved into a new general repair shop at Pico and Western in Los Angeles. He moved to yet another shop in 1938 at the corner of Venice and Crenshaw. That was also the year that his son Vic, Jr., was born. During all his moves, Bobby Meeks, Vic's able assistant, moved with him.

Vic became fascinated with midget racing and hot rodding at the dry lakes. He bought a 1932 Ford roadster to run on El Mirage dry lakes. His business partner was Tommy Thickston. They were both interested in going fast and in modified automobiles and they designed the first Edelbrock manifold. It was a 180-degree, single-carburetor manifold for a Ford flathead V–8. From this design came their next manifold, which used a pair of Stromberg 97 carburetors.

Vic was racing and testing his parts on his 1932 Ford roadster at El Mirage, some eighty miles east of Los Angeles, and he became a consistent winner. He even reached a top speed of 121 mph in the roadster. It was at about this time that he first started working on cylinder heads as well. Vic took cast iron

"Denver" heads, which were special, high-altitude heads and used a higher compression, and he filled and milled the head for a further increase in compression. This was a Band-Aid treatment and Vic knew it. And the only way to do it right was to cast his own alloy heads.

Vic continued working on his performance parts and fit the roadster with his prototypes. He would drive it to the lakes, remove the fenders and windscreen, then race the car, refitting the fenders and windshield for the drive home. 1940 was significant because that was the year Vic opened his own new shop by himself and went into the performance parts business for keeps.

His continual wins impressed other racers at the dry lakes, leading to requests for parts, mainly his twin-carburetor manifold for the V-8 Ford flathead, which was a 180-degree firing order design. He then designed and manufactured his first cast manifold, called the "Slingshot," for that same Ford V-8. This was the first product to feature the famous cast "EDELBROCK" block lettering. Only ten to fifteen of these manifolds were produced.

With the advent of World War II, Vic shelved his racing activities and used his machinist skills for the war effort, but not before he had been clocked at 121.42 mph in the fenderless, 32 roadster. He went to work in the shipyards at Long Beach, then at Douglas Aircraft, and then with Len Saleter as partner in a machine shop doing contract machine work for the war effort. Vic learned new skills and increased his perception of what he could build with the right machining tools and a good foundry.

Near the end of the war, he moved into a new facility in Hollywood. He was back in the general

Vic is shown in front of his shop with his matching speedway midgets.

repair business but worked on performance parts and engine building as a side line. Vic finally had the time to design his first high-compression alloy heads for flathead Fords. They met with immediate success at the dry lakes and in speedway racing. With the war ended and a solid business now starting to develop, Vic bought the performance industry's first engine dyno. It enabled him to perform scientific evaluations of the real performance gains of his designs.

By now, Vic had become strongly involved with midget car racing and his equipment was installed in almost every winning car. At one point, ten of eleven records were set with Edelbrock-equipped cars powered by Ford V-8-60s. Vic bought his first midget speedway car, which had been built by D. W. McCully. With Bobby Meeks as team manager

Vic poses with his 1932 roadster in this photo shot around 1946.

Vic, Sr., ran a test on a new small-block Chevy that was set up for a racing boat.

49

This gorgeous 1934 Ford was sponsored by Vic and bore the title of the Edelbrock Special.

and head wrench, they toured the L.A. speedways, racing as often as six nights a week. In late 1946, he bought a Kurtis Kraft midget and continued his racing. He had become known for fast flathead Fords and was building two to three V-8-60 midget engines for customers each month.

Business flourished and Vic finally built his first all-new shop, it was on Jefferson Boulevard in Los Angeles. He made racing pistons for many applica-

tions, and his shop was well-equipped with milling machinery to do things that, before the war, were unknown in building race car engines.

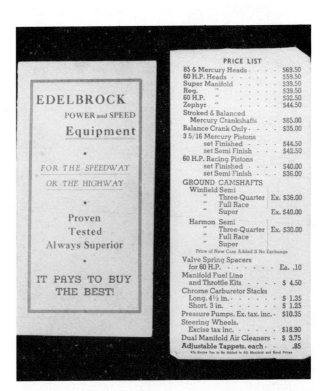

Vic, Jr. (left), and Vic, Sr. (right), posed in front of the Jefferson Boulevard factory.

The first Edelbrock catalogs were small, pocket-sized pamphlets, and they came with price lists. Heads were $69.50 and cams were $40 in the early days.

In the early-fifties dry lakes racing activities shifted partly to Bonneville. Edelbrock-equipped cars continued to win. The first single-engine car to go over 200 mph was Edelbrock-equipped. That was the Xydias-Bachelor Streamliner, and Vic continued to sponsor his midget at the speedway. The reputation of his performance parts had spread and a solid export business had opened up to Brazil for Ford V-8 60 parts.

Through the fifties his parts catalogue developed from a two-page flyer into a ten-page booklet, as Vic expanded his line of alloy heads, fly wheels, pistons, cams and adjustable tappets for Fords, Mercurys and Lincolns. His parts were sought in all forms of motorsports, from boat racers to sprint car drivers. His manifold selection increased to seven, including single, dual and triple Stromberg set-ups.

Vic continued to develop his ideas on drag racing engines. He contributed his time and energy to unify the performance parts industry, and helped others get their start. Cam manufacturer Ed Iskenderian is perhaps the most notable of these.

Vic researched overhead-valve intake manifolds with his dyno and in 1956, conducted the first in-depth evaluation of the new Chevy 265. The results of these tests were published in *Hot Rod* magazine, giving the reader access to information never before available. Edelbrock continued developments on the Ford 312, 352 and others. By now he was producing a wide range of street and racing intake manifold applications. At the Orange Bowl Regatta, an Edelbrock-equipped Chevy powerboat cleaned up the championship.

He was working on ideas no other manufacturer was even considering. He started the first parts warehousing program, which let a number of manufacturers make their parts available from one source. It developed into a large operation, but under pressures from the manufacturing side of the Edelbrock Corporation, Vic discontinued his involvement to concentrate on production. Vic may have ended his role in the concept, but it was already established as the foundation of the major distribution system used today in the performance industry.

Ozzie Osborne's 1929 A roadster was powered by an Edelbrock-equipped Ford flathead.

Vic, Sr. (left), with Vic, Jr.

1961 was a year of further breakthroughs. Vic produced the first Ram Log Manifold, a six-carb setup for the street and strip that worked with the 283 and 327 Chevy. Also emerging from this work was the cross-ram manifold, which became the forerunner of the performance manifolds of the eighties.

Just when he was beginning to see the gratifying results of his hard work, Vic Edelbrock, Sr., died, a victim of cancer, at the age of forty-nine. He was held in high esteem by all who knew him.

Just like his father, Vic, Jr., held a special vision of a great future for his family name, and he stepped up to take over the reigns as head of the company. He had been at his father's side, watching and learning, and had shown a natural affinity for engines. Like his father, Vic, Jr., assembled a team of talented people on his staff. The combination of these specialists and Vic, Jr.'s, flair has since developed "Edelbrock" into the biggest and most respected name in the performance industry—an outstanding achievement for a father and son team that has its roots in a shop fire in Kansas more than sixty years ago.

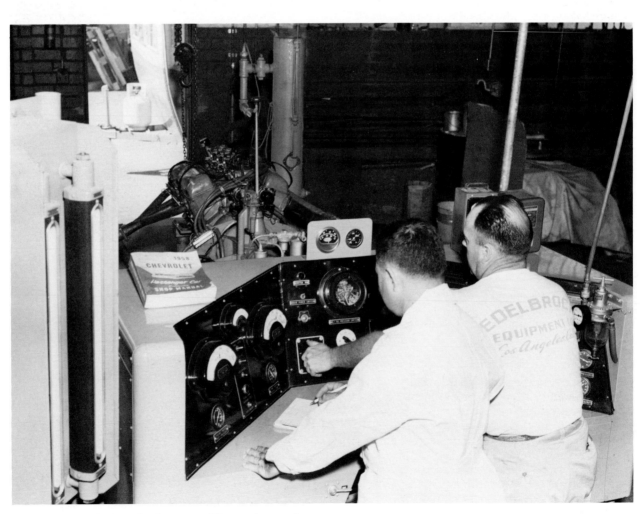

The Edelbrock dyno at the factory on Vernon Avenue is shown testing a 1958 Chevy 283 engine.

Chapter 9

Don Garlits

Drag racing is one of those motorsports lucky enough to have been blessed with an all-time legend. Stock car racing has its ultimate legend in "The King," Richard Petty. Indy car racing has that tough ol' Texan, A. J. Foyt. Drag racing has a man who was an innovator, a determined—call it stubborn, if you will—individual and a winner of legendary proportions: "Big Daddy" Don Garlits.

Like Petty and Foyt, Garlits has made such an indelible mark on his sport that even if someone eventually breaks all of his records and wins more races, Big Daddy will never be forgotten. He'll always be at the top of the list among drag racers.

Born on January 14, 1932, to Prussian parents, Donald Glenn Garlits' early years were filled with school and a love of mechanical devices. He graduated from high school and studied accounting. His first job was with the Mass Brothers Department Store in Tampa, Florida, but the dull, routine nature of accounting soon had him looking for other careers. His stepfather, Alex Weir, suggested that he change occupations "only if you first find a job that is going to keep you happy in life." Consequently, Don opened his shop, "Don's Garage," with the help of his brother, Ed, in Tampa. Business flourished, and he eventually changed the name to "Don's Speed Shop."

Don was a keen street racer in Tampa, and when the opportunity to try drag racing came along in 1951, he headed for the first drag race event at the Zephyrhills Airport in Florida. The drag racing bug bit him hard and he became a regular competitor. He worked as a mechanic at his shop during the day and built his cars at night to race on weekends. As his drag racing calendar started filling up, he gradually handed over all the shop work to his brother.

In 1953, he married Pat and "retired" from drag racing, but the need for speed had him back on the track a year later with his 1950 Ford family car.

Don waves from the cockpit of an old front-engine dragster after winning a Winternationals title at Pomona. The well-soiled palm shows that he was his own chief mechanic.

Don started taking his weekend racing seriously and built a stripped-down 1927 Ford T-roadster for the track. This racer quickly evolved into the first Florida "slingshot" dragster. Don used it to win the 1955 Safety Safari meet at Lake City, Florida. This was the first of hundreds of trophies he would win from the NHRA over the next thirty years.

Don's innovative style and interest in safety started early. In 1955, he replaced the front wheels on his racer with motorcycle wheels to give the semi-slingshot a lighter front end and a better elapsed time.

In 1956, he built a tube-frame slingshot dragster and in March headed for the Famoso Drag Strip at Bakersfield, California. He called the car "Swamp Rat," and it was made from a set of 1930 Chevy frame rails, a 1954 Chrysler Hemi, a Crower U-Fab intake manifold and six Stromberg carburetors.

With this dragster, Don cleaned up the local Top Eliminator competition in Florida and then headed for Bakersfield, where sixty-four dragsters had entered the East-West showdown created especially for Don's first west coast appearance.

It was a love-hate relationship with the crowd and spectators. They did not like "the kid" from Tampa coming out to the west coast to show them how to win on the quarter-mile. They heckled him with "Tampa Don" and "Garbage Don," threw beer cans and shouted insults. Events such as this thickened his skin for the coming years. Don knew he could beat the competition on this strip but he did not win that time. He *did* assure them he would be back to show them one day "just how it's done." He showed them three times, with new cars and more experience, in 1965, 1967 and 1971, when he won the U.S. Fuel and Gas Championships. Then there were no hecklers, just cheers and shouts from the appreciative crowds in the stands.

Don continued racing Swamp Rat around the country as his business permitted. In 1957, he added a hypoid rear end and extended the wheelbase, making Swamp Rat even more competitive. Don's mechanical and driving skills made a perfect combination. He could tune the car and then drive it, feeling just how much difference his changes had made.

Back in Florida, Don continued racing Swamp Rat and in early 1959, he ran the unheard-of speed of 180 mph. Even with this hot time under his belt, however, 1959 proved to be a hard year. At Chester, South Carolina, in June, a blower explosion on his front-engined dragster caused him massive burns, but the Swamp Rat toughed it out and returned to the track within months.

Don and his family moved to Troy, Michigan, in 1960 so Don could be closer to Chrysler, but after his father died he moved back to the family ranch in central Florida in 1966. There, he opened "Hi-Performance World," a speed shop.

His high-speed East Coast runs attracted the attention of the West Coast track operators and they issued a cross-country challenge: $50,000 win-or-lose appearance money for three winter races in Califor-

Here is the Garlits Wynns-Liner, a Dodge-powered car with a body shaped by Jocko Johnson.

nia and Arizona. Garlits accepted, quit his regular jobs and hit the road as one of drag racing's first professional racers. It was not an easy life. Being on the road every summer weekend added up to 85,000 miles every year and meant grinding out a living at a sport that had once been the bane of every police department in the country.

His ability to deal with the physical side of drag racing was again tested to the limit in 1965, when he crashed badly and broke his back. His recovery took months, but his ideas for and dedication to the sport continued as he developed his driving touch and fine-tuned his car-building skills.

Don built thirty-one dragsters, all called Swamp Rat. In virtually all cases they were hemi-powered, and for many years, he ran with Dodge sponsorship. All of his later cars used hemi-derivative drag racing engines.

Don's ability to go faster increased as he tried and worked with new and innovative materials, people and equipment. His prime requirement has always been to have a safe car—but sometimes it takes a sudden jolt to bring to light the dangerous potentials of the sport. Don was a leading figure in making drag racing safer. His concern for safety came to a peak on March 8, 1970 when he ran at Long Beach, California, in the AHRA (American Hot Rod Association) Grand American series. Driving his front-engined dragster, he came smoking out of the trap before the transmission exploded, breaking the dragster in half and badly crippling his right foot in one of the sport's most spectacular accidents.

Don smoked the tires of the Dart 2, an open-topped funny car, during a burnout.

This accident made him think, and at the beginning of the 1971 season, Don was back with a rear-engined dragster that virtually kept all mechanical dangers away from the driver. Amid heckling from the competition that the idea was just a gimmick, Don made them believers at Gainesville, Florida, with an elapsed time of 6.26 seconds—the first car quicker than 6.5 seconds. This car established the rear-engine design as the standard for future top fuel racers.

This is Don's famous Wynn's Jammer, a front-engined top fueler.

This is the famous Navy-sponsored top fuel racer. Note the fish logo, a religious symbol, mounted near the nose of the car.

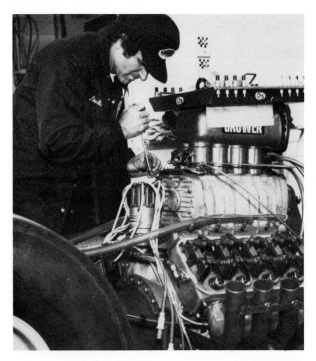

Don was always his own machinist and mechanic. He designed and produced his own parts and took a hands-on approach to his racing so he knew the cars were prepared to his demanding standards.

Don's stunning ability with the dragster put him on covers of magazines, on TV shows, and when he challenged a Phantom jet fighter on the deck of the USS Lexington, he was featured on U.S. Navy recruiting posters. His military connections continued when he toured Vietnam as an entertainment celebrity. Don wrote of his anti-Vietnam views in an issue of *Hot Rod* magazine, and when he met President Nixon at a White House reception, did not hesitate to tell the President to "bring our boys home."

Don's dedication to drag racing has made him a legend among legends. His operation was always low-key, with minimal fuss and maximum precision. His days on the road, driving cross-country from track to track and home again, sometimes took him 2,000 miles in three days.

Those times taught Don the keys to success: work hard, run top-rate equipment and win. The Garlits mystique was striking; when he arrived for a major race, the entire track was instantly on notice: "Big Daddy's here!"

Don grew accustomed to the attention and turned it to his advantage. He could psyche out the opposition; they knew that just to qualify, they would have to run against the "Old Master." This gave him a decisive advantage over the younger racers but not one that could guarantee success, by any means.

His consistent style helped him earn more than seven million dollars in purse money, thanks to a true team effort. It has taken the combined efforts of his wife Pat, his daughters Donna and Gay Lyn, his crew chiefs Herb Parks and Ron Barrow, Tommy (T. C.) Lemons, Marvin Schwartz, Ed Garlits, Connie Swingle and his business partner, Art Malone.

The size of drag racing purses today is partly due to the battles Don waged with both the NHRA and AHRA over the years. He has been called everything from hero to outlaw during his career, but he has always fought for safer tracks and better pay for drivers and owners.

It's been said that Don Garlits is a tough man who's hard on his competitors and even tougher on the track. His view of the world of hot rodding and drag racing has come from nearly forty years of being first across the line. He has been controversial, always willing to try something new and hard as nails to beat.

Don has always cared about what is going on around him and has not cared much about what folks thought about him or his ways. Because of his strong belief in God, he painted a cross and the words "God is Love" across the cowl of his dragsters. It was a statement that took courage to make, since it lost him sponsors and produced a rash of heat from his competitors.

Don first retired from the pro circuit in 1980 to concentrate on his museum project in Ocala, Florida. During the next four years, he continued match racing, and in 1985 and 1986, he came back from retirement and won the Nationals both times.

To expand on his winning accomplishments in drag racing would take another book. However, Don Garlits' list of racing firsts, national champion-

Big Daddy exits the bleach box during a big burnout before a run of 6.10 seconds with a top speed of 244 mph.

Flames shoot from the pipes as Don gets ready to make a run under the lights at the 1973 Springnationals.

This is Don's Swamp Rat XXX in action at the NHRA Gatornationals at Gainesville, Florida. The streamlined nose design and small front wheels paid off as they helped Don to a record run of 272.56 mph.

ship wins and world records shows that he has spent his life building a reputation as the winningest racing car driver of all time.

Don retired from competition after his second famous "flight" totaled "Swamp Rat XXX" on August 21, 1987, during a run at Spokane, Washington. It was a spectacular way to end his career.

He'd had thirty-eight years of serious drag racing. His thirty-three Swamp Rats have been towed through Canada, Mexico, England and Australia. He has won practically every drag race worth winning, more times than anybody else, and faster than all the younger guys.

Don Garlits is the epitome of a sportsman, yet he is a tough and rather withdrawn person who has always preferred to work far away from much of drag racing's "fast" crowd.

In retirement, Don is still very active. He works on promotional events; races at Bonneville; does TV commentary on drag racing; runs his museum with the help of Pat and his staff; and still enjoys racing some of his older Swamp Rats at nostalgia drag racing events across the nation.

Today, he lives in Ocala on the grounds of his "Don Garlits Museum of Drag Racing," which houses the crown jewels of drag racing, from the earliest slingshots to the last of the Swamp Rats. It's all there, all part of the legend of Don Garlits, the Champion's Champion.

A Garlits family shot of Don, his wife Pat and their daughters, Donna and Gay Lyn.

Don Garlits Career Highlights

Racing Firsts
1957 — First dragster to run over 170 mph, Brooksville, Florida (176.40)
1958 — First dragster to run 180 mph, Brooksville, Florida (180)
1961 — First dragster to run "7–second" E.T., Columbia, South Carolina (7.88)
1964 — First dragster to run 200 mph, Great Meadows, New Jersey (201.34)
1966 — First Funny Car to run 200 mph, St. Petersburg, Florida (200.44)
1968 — First dragster to run 240 mph, Alton, Illinois (240)
1971 — First dragster to run below 6.30 E.T., Gainesville, Florida (6.26)
1972 — First dragster to run 6.10 E.T., Niagara Falls, New York
1973 — First dragster to run in "5s" back-to-back, Portland, Oregon (5.95)
1975 — First dragster to break 250 mph, Ontario, Canada (250.69)
1977 — First dragster to break 255 mph, Englishtown, New Jersey (255.68)
1979 — First dragster to run 252 mph back-to-back
1979 — First dragster to run over 200 mph in the ⅛ mile (204.24)

1982 — First Top Fuel to run over 260 mph (260.49 & 260.49)
1985 — First to run over 265 mph (265.48)
1986 — First NHRA dragster to run over 270 mph, Gainesville, Florida (272.56)
1986 — First to repeat back-to-back NHRA Top Fuel World Championships

Technical Innovations
1955 — First to use bike front wheels on dragster
1957 — First to use hypoid rear end
1957 — First to experiment with extended wheelbase
1965 — First to use port injection on dragster
1971 — First to develop championship rear-engine dragster
1971 — First to use four-disc clutch
1985 — First to use frontal ground effects

NHRA — Nationals Titles
North Star Nationals — 1986
Summernationals — 1985
Winternationals — 1963, 1971, 1973, 1975, 1987
Gatornationals — 1972, 1977, 1978, 1986
Springnationals — 1968, 1971, 1979
U.S. Nationals — 1964, 1967, 1968, 1975, 1978, 1984, 1985, 1986
Supernationals — 1973, 1974
Grandnationals — Moison — 1975, 1985

World Finals — 1975, 1979, 1984
Points Championship — 1975, 1985, 1986
Safety Safari — 1958
Fall Nationals — 1979
Southern Nationals — 1985
Cajun Nationals — 1985, 1986
Keystone Nationals — 1985
Chief Auto Parts Nationals — 1986

IHRA Nationals Titles
Winston Nationals — 1977
Winterclassic — 1976
Springnationals — 1972, 1975
Winternationals — 1972, 1975, 1979
U.S. Nationals — 1973, 1976
World Nationals — 1975, 1976, 1977
Pro-Am Nationals — 1975, 1978
Summernationals — 1975, 1976, 1977
All American Nationals — 1975, 1976
Points Championship — 1975, 1976, 1977, 1978
Dixie Nationals — 1976, 1977, 1979
Winston World Champion — 1975, 1976, 1977, 1978
Northern Nationals — 1977, 1978, 1979
World Finals — 1978

AHRA — Nationals Titles
Gateway Nationals — 1972, 1973, 1978, 1979, 1980, 1981, 1982, 1983
Nationals — 1971, 1972, 1973, 1974, 1979, 1983
Winternationals — 1970, 1973, 1978, 1981, 1982, 1983
Springnationals — 1970, 1973, 1978, 1979, 1980, 1982, 1984
Summernationals — 1958, 1966, 1978, 1979, 1980, 1984
Northern Nationals — 1972, 1973, 1974
Southern Nationals — 1971, 1972, 1973, 1974
Orange County Grand National — 1974
Grand Prix of Mexico — 1972
World Finals — 1971, 1972, 1973, 1979, 1982, 1984
World Championship — 1969, 1971, 1972, 1973
World Points Champion — 1971, 1972, 1973, 1974, 1978, 1979, 1980, 1982, 1983, 1984
Mello Yello Nationals — 1979
Ozark Nationals — 1979
Chi-Town Nationals — 1983

Chapter 10

C. J. Hart

The old saying that "Nobody's a native Californian" was much closer to the truth back in the forties, when thousands of families packed up and moved west to see if the West Coast really was the land of opportunity.

That meant that when California hot rodders and street racers stopped their engines to shoot the bull, they frequently learned that their highway rivals came from similar roots in the Midwest and East.

A 1937 Ford coupe and a Deuce roadster pair off at the Santa Ana Drags in August 1952, and C.J. flags them off.

One such man was Cloyce J. "C.J." Hart, who moved his family west after being blackballed at a Findlay, Ohio, Ford dealership and losing his job. He and his wife Peggy packed and piled into their Mercury sedan with their two children for the five-day drive to a new hometown, Santa Ana, California.

It's ironic that the drive west took C.J. and the family along highways that were frequented by hotshoe hot rodders. The irony is that C.J.'s involvement in motorsports would eventually move those racers off those roads and earn him fame as "the hero who turned street racing into drag racing."

It was 1943 when the Harts reached Santa Ana, a city that would be their home for the next forty years. A Ford dealership on the main street needed a mechanic, and within days of first pulling into town, C.J. had a new job and a new start.

C. J.'s new life included fooling around with hot rods. Street racing was popular and C. J. was more than a casual observer. Once the war was over, dry lakes racing revived and C. J. took to racing like a duck takes to water.

Soon C.J. and his friends sought ways to go racing closer to home. The war had left California dotted with many unused military bases covered with concrete parking lots and runways. One of these was known as the Mile Square, a square mile of concrete paving. It was part of a Navy base in Orange County. C. J. and his buddies spent time there on weekends, running off up to eight abreast. "It was one of those situations where you could nearly always beat *someone*," according to C. J. After a few months, however, they were stopped by a company of base Marines with fixed bayonets.

The adventure sparked C. J.'s mind, however. He and his buddies still wanted to race and decided to look for a place to run flat out—legally. It took several months to get things in order, but with the backing of Creighton Hunter and Frank Stillwell, C. J. approached the management of the Santa Ana municipal airport. They agreed to lease one of the unused runways every Sunday but said Hart would have to provide separate insurance and the airport would take 10% of the gate receipts. The three partners chipped in $500 each and the "Santa Ana Drags" were in business. Hunter dropped out two weeks after the first event, leaving C. J. and Stillwell to run the show.

The track opened on a hot summer's night June 19, 1950, with about fifty-five entries and three-hundred spectators. It cost fifty cents to watch or race, and all the organizing was done by volunteers. Times were clocked with a couple of stopwatches and C. J. had a few small trophies on hand for the winners.

Although C. J. didn't race, his wife Peggy became a regular drag racer, well known for her speed and reaction time. At first, she raced the family Cadillac, but moved quickly on to a 1927 T flathead roadster. She became a feature attraction at the races and "the woman to beat." C. J. built her a Cadillac-powered rail on a Model A frame. He set it up with a roll bar hoop and Peggy did the rest. C. J. preferred the lakes and Bonneville. He built numerous lakes cars with his favorite combination of using

His trademark stogie in hand, C.J. flags off a pair of GM rivals at Santa Ana.

C.J. with his cigar at the Orange County Raceway office in 1971.

62

a Ford-powered Cadillac motor. In 1955, C. J. took his new Thunderbird to the salt; it was powered by a relatively stock Cadillac ohv engine and ran 119 mph.

The hot rod racing scene was bitterly divided between traditional dry lakes racers and the stockers. C. J.'s Santa Ana Drags catered mostly to street cars but, nonetheless, he invited the lakes racers to bring their cars and their timing equipment to his events. They refused. C. J. then devised a new timing system and installed his own set of clocks that could read out to a top speed of 149.75 mph.

Classes for the races were divided by measuring weight over rear axle ratio. Don Parks and C. J. devised this system as the easiest way to calibrate just how fast each car could run. As elapsed time was not the governing number for the racers, the tech crew could check the rear axle ratio by jacking up the car and measuring the rear wheel run-out against a rotation of the tailshaft.

Word got out that the Santa Ana Drags were a hot ride, and eventually the lakes racers started coming down for "a Sunday drive." At first, C. J. didn't have a class for them but he quickly made it a lucrative event. He would pay $1 per mile over 130 mph. His Top Eliminator final purse ran to $155 one Sunday in 1959.

Looking back on Santa Ana, C. J. recalled, "I didn't invent drag racing; that sort of thing's been going on ever since there were cars. I just got it off the streets."

Peggy Hart, C.J.'s wife, was one of C.J.'s early drivers. Here she straps on her helmet before a run in her Cadillac-powered rail.

Creighton Hunter, one of the original Santa Ana Drags owners, pulls on a helmet as he prepares to race his famous Mooneyes Turtle-deck T.

However you look at it, C. J.'s most significant credit should read, "The inventor of the commercial dragstrip."

C. J. and Stillwell ran the drags efficiently and safely for nine years, but the rapid expansion of Orange County led to calls for the expansion of the Santa Ana Airport, which would return the runway to full-time use. The Santa Ana Drags had become world famous, even being covered with a feature in *Life* magazine, but time and the tide of progress were against the track.

Today, the old Santa Ana dragstrip is part of John Wayne International Airport in southwestern Orange County. You can watch the planes land and take off where Garlits, Thompson, Ivo, Nancy and others first gave a meaning to the term "ET."

C. J. moved on to promoting a new night racing event in Taft, California. This event lasted only a few months. Bakersfield was only fifty miles away and once the track management saw how well C. J. was doing with his nighttime event, they jumped on the wagon, and C. J. lost out to the established Bakersfield track. Never a man to sit still, C. J. opened a used car lot in Santa Ana, which he ran for several years.

His great attraction to drag racing was still gnawing at him. In 1965, Mickey Thompson asked him to take over as manager of the Lions Association Drag Strip (LADS) in Wilmington, near Long Beach. Lions was operated by a management team from six Lions Clubs, with each club having two members on the board. C. J.'s first directive was to make each Sunday an amateur racers' day.

Lions had a reputation as the best drag racing facility in the country. It hosted weekly shows with all categories of dragsters: AA/Fuel, Altereds, Top Gassers, Jet Cars, Super Stocks and eventually Funny Cars. Saturday night was always the premier show, and all through these years, C. J. kept his admission at $3 even when $5 was the regular price elsewhere.

Lions offered class action for the part-time racer every Sunday, plus car club events and an early form of ET bracket racing. C. J.'s innovative ideas for the "regular" guys developed a "bracket" program to group racers according to half-second increments in brackets between eleven and seventeen seconds. This heads-up racing offered trophies for winners of all twelve ET brackets. It was also the year that C. J. started paying cash purses to run-off winners.

At Lions, C. J. ran events Saturdays and Sundays, plus his famous Wednesday "grudge race

Creighton Hunter's T was a popular car and would pair off against all comers. Here he runs against a Studebaker sedan in August 1952.

C.J. gives a hug to Linda Vaughan as the Thrush Girls pose with some track officials at a 1988 NHRA event.

64

night," for eight years. He enjoyed the job immensely but in mid-1971, he resigned because he was fed up with some of his supervisors on the Lions Club board of directors. There was one in particular who, he said, attended the board meetings drunk and obnoxious. "Can't stand drunks. Never could, never would," said C. J. A year-and-a-half later, Lions was closed.

C. J. tried to retire in 1973, but the love of drag racing was still deep within him. For a while, he worked at the Orange County International Raceway. He also did consultant work with promoters seeking his expertise at major events.

It didn't take long for the American Hot Rod Association to ask C. J. to become its events manager. His new job as supervisor meant he was responsible to set up, tear down and run all AHRA drag racing events. He worked diligently at this until 1979.

In 1980, his wife Peggy passed away. C. J. was despondent over her death. "I didn't know what to

do. I would go to bed not ever wanting to wake up again." But his friends at the NHRA offered him a job. They needed a man who knew drag racing. They also wanted someone to drive the track dryer and move it from track to track.

C. J. was overjoyed at the idea. He rolled out his motorhome, hooked up the track dryer and headed out to cover the NHRA circuit for nine consecutive seasons.

Today, C. J. is very active for a man of around eighty years old. He works in a hardware store in Elsinore, California, three days a week and hopes to return to the NHRA circuit as one of the crew for the next few seasons. He still loves "the smell of burnt rubber and fuel in the morning" and, as the end of the century approaches, one of the great golden oldies is enjoying his "retirement years" working the track and remaining part of a sport that he helped create when the law and common sense made street racing a sport of the past.

A flamed 1932 Hiboy is towed to the line at Santa Ana, ready for its appointment with the time clocks.

Chapter 11

Joe Hunt

Joe Hunt was one of those lucky men who got to spend more time at racetracks than any other place during his life. If he wasn't at a track to enjoy a race, he was there to learn what was new or, during his productive automotive career, to help improve the technology of the machines being raced.

It's fortunate for several generations of racers that Joe broke away from the tracks long enough to become an expert aircraft mechanic because the knowledge he brought from the airstrip to the racetrack greatly improved racing ignitions and improve the competition.

Joe (standing) got his first taste of high performance when he went to Indy to work on the pit crew for the Marks- *Miller Special, which was driven by George Connor. Connor finished nineteenth in the 500 in 1935.*

Joe was a race fan from the start, and as a kid he loved to hang off the corner rail at the speedway and let the cars spray dirt in his face. He grew up in southwest Los Angeles so he had plenty of area tracks to visit to get his fill of high-speed action. When he couldn't make it to the tracks, he followed the action via radio broadcasts because even as a youngster, he was hooked on fast machines and dirt racing. He was a good student and attended Manual Arts High School in Los Angeles from 1933 until 1936, playing hot rodder with his 1932 hi-boy roadster after school with the likes of Ed Iskenderian and Vic Edelbrock. After graduating, he attended Cal Flyers, an aviation trade school for aircraft maintenance engineers, mechanics and airframe and flight crews, and became a qualified aviation mechanic.

His fascination with auto racing took him to the dry lakes and the speedway, and in 1938, he went to Indy as part of the pit crew for the Marks-Miller Special driven by George Connor. The roadster was powered by a four-cylinder Miller engine and placed nineteenth, with an average speed of 120 mph.

Joe returned to Indy a year later, still working on the pit crew but with greater dreams and hopes in mind. During his time on the pit crew, he realized that many of the non-finishers had failed due to the lack of a race-quality ignition. This realization was the "spark" that ten years later would put a Joe Hunt Magneto on virtually every race car at Indy.

In 1940, Joe entered Indy with his own car for his first try for the 500. Johnny Parsons was his driver, but they failed to qualify. World War II interrupted the racing and Joe was called to serve as a civilian flight inspector in Greenland and England. His knowledge of aircraft engines expanded dramatically and he discovered how well built and reliable aircraft magnetos really were, especially compared to those in automobiles.

With the war over, Joe returned to California and civilian life. For a while, he was rebuilding automotive engines. He ran a sprint car, with Johnny Parsons doing the wheel work. They raced the tracks in both northern and southern California with a Dodge six-power racer.

In 1948, he qualified as a flight engineer for TWA. It was the beginning of a long, professional career that would support his "hobby," as Joe called his company (Joe Hunt Magnetos), and his dream to win at Indy.

Within a year of taking the full-time position with TWA, Joe opened his magneto shop on Redon-

Joe was a flight engineer for TWA. He is shown deboarding from his regular east-west Constellation run. It was his aviation background that helped him improve automotive magnetos so greatly.

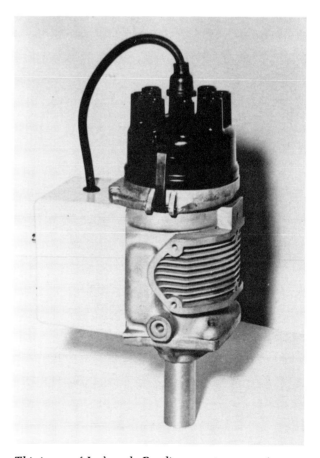

This is one of Joe's early Bendix magneto conversions.

do Beach Boulevard as a sideline to help him promote and nurture his intense interest in racing. His experience with aviation magnetos had given him a clear-cut vision that the same type of magneto could be used on a racing engine.

The quality of automotive magnetos left much to be desired. Joe worked until he perfected a magneto that would not fly apart at high rpm. His first prototype was fitted to Johnny McDowell's midget racer. McDowell had been experiencing ignition trouble for months and was apparently delighted to try something new. Joe's new magneto helped him win four out of seven first places in the first week.

Joe's ideas were considered adventurous by many racers, but with his old friend and driver, Johnny Parsons, running his modified magneto at Indy in 1949, along with four other qualifiers, Joe's status as "the Sultan of Spark" suddenly had new meaning.

Parsons became a test pilot for Joe Hunt Magnetos and in 1950, he won "The Great Race" equipped with a Hunt Magneto. By 1955, every starter at Indy was fitted with one of Joe's magnetos, and they became the standard ignition system on many of the winning cars for the next fifteen years.

In 1952, Joe moved his shop to Vernon Avenue in Los Angeles because he needed more space. His magnetos were sought by speedway racers, lakes drag racers, motorcycle racers and the street crowd, as well as the entire field at Indy. Joe's magneto set-up provided the most reliable spark source and could be adapted to any racing engine.

Joe used his vacation time to set up shop at Indy. He had his test equipment on hand and spent his time calibrating his customers' magnetos. He was proud of his work. When, on one occasion, a Hunt Magneto was blamed for a car dropping out of a race, Joe stormed over to Gasoline Alley, retrieved the magneto and ran it on his test gear. It checked out perfectly. The next day, when the team tore the motor down, the problem was traced to a stuck valve.

A simple, straightforward ad from the early days, one which was familiar to many hot rodders.

Joe (left) works with his father on some test equipment at the Vernon Avenue factory.

With spectators' cars parked inside the turn, Keith Andrews powers the Joe Hunt Magneto car up Pikes Peak in 1954, the year it won the title.

Initially, Joe was taking Bendix aviation magnetos and converting them to automotive use with new cam drive adaptors, special clamps and graduated scales for acute adjustments. He figured that the high-rpm, long-duration flying the Bendix magnetos had done during the war ably demonstrated their inherent reliability. All he needed to do was adapt them for automotive use and get the same performance factors working for him. Joe tested and calibrated the magnetos in a full-scale lab he had built.

His product lines included magnetos for V–8–90 Fords, Offys, Drakes, Millers and virtually any other engine that the speedway, lakes and Indy drivers wanted to use. The Offy staff was so impressed with Joe's magnetos that his products were made standard components for all factory engines.

Joe then discovered a new source: the famous Swiss-built Vertex Scintilla magnetos. His switch from Bendix to the Vertex became his winning edge.

Along with his annual pilgrimages to Indy, Joe was drawn to a special mountain in Colorado to the hunt for a win: Pikes Peak. Joe ran a Rail Dirt Championship car powered by an Offy for four years, and Pikes Peak proved to be the greatest racing

achievement of any of his sponsored cars. In 1953, Joe's car placed third, in 1954, his car number twenty-seven won; in 1955, he placed sixth.

Indy, however, was his greatest love. From 1951 until 1981, Joe annually entered one of his cars under the banner of "Joe Hunt Magnetos." His cars became as common as the Watson roadster at the Brickyard. It would seem that for the time, effort and capital investment Joe put into his Indy effort, he didn't get much back in the way of success. In thirty years of trying, his cars qualified only twice, in 1960 and 1971. He enjoyed the challenge, however, and derived great personal satisfaction from being part of the Indy scene.

Surprisingly, his greatest contribution to Indy was his faith in drivers he called "the young new bulls." Joe employed Bobby and Al Unser, Gary Bettenhausen, Johnny Parsons, Jimmy Daywalt and Dan "Termite" Jones. Many drivers were given their first try at the 500 in a Joe Hunt Magneto Special. Joe also co-sponsored Indy cars with Wynn's.

Through the years, the Hunt company developed a wide range of applications for the Vertex Scintilla magnetos. The drag racing community

That's Joe at right, celebrating the 1954 Pikes Peak win. Next to him is his wife Mary, and their son Tommy is at the *far left. The driver was Keith Andrews, who died in a practice session at Indy in 1957.*

came to rely on Joe and his magnetos, and they became as common as slicks on a dragster. Chris Karamesines, "The Golden Greek," was one of Joe's regular customers. Every NHRA Nationals winner from the mid-sixties through the mid-eighties ran a Hunt Magneto, as did the USAC sprint car racers.

The company still produces thousands of racing magnetos for every form of four-wheel and boat racing motorsport. Joe's son Tommy recalls watching his father work hard to achieve his dreams. "Many times my father would try to do too much with too little. He would go beyond reason, sometimes failing because he was pushing the limits of his engines too far. I remember he lost a big race because he tried to get 'one more race' out of a $25 clutch disc." Joe was reluctant to ask for help even though he was generous with his own time and energy.

Tommy left the family business and became a successful sprint car driver of championship standing during the mid- to late-seventies.

Through the years, Joe's wife Mary worked as his business manager at the three different locations as the company grew and moved. Joe retired from TWA in 1976 at age sixty. He had flown on pistons and turbo props and had worked into the jet age before he retired as the most senior flight engineer on TWA's 747 fleet.

Since then, Joe has managed his company full-time, but in 1981, he asked Tommy to take over. Tommy hesitated at first, and agreed only if he could move it to Rancho Cordova in northern California. Tommy and his wife continue to operate Hunt Magnetos, and he serves as USAC's vice president of western operations. Joe, who had led a relatively healthy life, succumbed to cancer and passed away in 1985.

Joe mixed his flight engineering background with a good dose of hot rodder's ingenuity to develop a line of ignition products that helped win more races than virtually any other single ignition product ever.

Many racers owe their success to this small company not only because Joe Hunt knew how to put a spark in the right place at the right time but because of his desire to help "those young bulls" get started. The "Sultan of Spark" always made sure that his magnetos were the best. He knew that those racers on the track needed all the dependable help they could get.

The setting at Pikes Peak is gorgeous, but the challenge of pushing a car to its limits during a climb can be intimidat- *ing. Joe and his driver survey the mountain prior to the 1954 race, which Joe's entry won.*

Chapter 12

Ermie Immerso

Ermie Immerso has had a career that is the envy of motorsports fans and racers everywhere. Sure, he grew up interested in cars and racing, but who didn't? The difference is that Ermie pursued his interest, developed his skills and earned one of the most impressive reputations in the automotive world to create opportunities for himself.

Those opportunities are many and varied, and include this enviable—but greatly abridged—list: he became a member of the 200 MPH Club by running 265 mph on the Bonneville Salt Flats; he helped field several entries into the Indy 500 over the years; he worked with Carroll Shelby on his famous Cobras, Mustangs and the King Cobra; he developed the power for a championship offshore boat racing team; and he created breathtaking cars that twice won the coveted Oakland Roadster Show's top prize.

Ermie's success is a tribute to a man taking advantage of his skills and interests and developing them so doors of opportunity are opened before him.

Ermie was a child of the pre-Depression years. He was born in New York in 1925, and his family moved to Phoenix, Arizona, where Ermie lived for the next thirty years. The son of a dairy farmer, Ermie was always tinkering with machinery. He had his first wheels by the time he was thirteen: a motor scooter that carted him four miles to school. But the need for speed got him started looking for a car.

Within a year, he had bought his first roadster, a 1928 Chevy. It was the first and last Chevy Ermie owned. Some of his friends' parents had midget racers which were all Ford-powered, and Ermie came to learn their strengths and weaknesses. He saw the same performance potential that every hot rodder saw in the Fords.

The Chevy was soon gone, replaced by a Model A roadster. Ermie set about using all his newly

acquired knowledge of midget race cars to modify the Model A. What he did must have created quite a storm, because he ran one of the fastest A's around. But others were pushing the speed envelope, too, because street racing was much in vogue around Phoenix at the time. The area's open desert roads were right for many a late-night foray, racing neck-

Ermie built this "tank" just for fun, and ran it at Bonneville in 1956. It was impressive, posting a top speed of 217 mph. It had a 354-ci alcohol Hemi with Hilborn injection and a T-33 belly tank.

Ermie raced the Mesa Jewelry Store Special, a dirt track T racer, for three years with considerable success.

Ermie was not just a racer. He also built this clean, custom Mercury, too, and it became his daily driver.

Crates held the four Ford 427 engines in place as Ermie worked on his Kraft Auto Special streamliner.

and-neck where the sheriff wouldn't try to police street racing activities.

Ermie was grassroots hot rod stuff. He lavished much attention on the A and had it running near peak performance, but soon other rodders had Cragar and Riley four-port heads. Ermie wanted power and decided to follow what the Californian rodders were doing by installing a 1937 21–stud, Ford V–8 flathead in his A—not just a stock flathead but one nicely warmed over. He milled and filled the heads to increase compression, added a downdraft carburetor and traded lots of parts and labor for a genuine Winfield cam. "The Ford ran pretty good. I could blow most of the competition into the weeds," remembered Ermie.

Not content with the car's looks, he took off the fenders. He wanted a California-style roadster. His next roadster was a 1929 Ford over a 1932 frame, powered by a V–8 "Flatty" with dual carbs, three-quarters race cam and a stroker crank. By this time, World War II was looming its ugly head over Ermie. At eighteen, he was drafted into the Navy as an aviation machinist's mate. His love of all things mechanical continued unabated. While serving on an aircraft carrier, he managed to learn much about fabrication and engines.

Ermie had stored the 1929 roadster without draining the motor and upon his return found that the alloy heads had frozen head studs. It took him hours to chisel them off. On weeknights he cruised the Coffee Pot Drive-In in Phoenix looking for a little race action. He would usually get at least one good run a night, and the sheriff didn't bother the boys as long as they were in the country and not racing on city streets.

His need for speed was growing. Ermie built a new rod for a daily driver. Using a 1936 Ford roadster, he assembled a 21–stud flathead with a McCullough supercharger and styled the roadster with a new, chopped Carson top. This, however, still did not fulfill his speed appetite.

A Track T roadster was his next rod, one which became a three-season runner. Ermie dubbed her the "Mesa Jewelry Store Special." Not happy with his abilities behind the wheel, he moved out of the driver's seat and took up engine building.

The G.I. Bill took him through auto upholstery school, paying his tuition and giving him a small living allowance. His natural abilities with his hands and his creative mind soon had him turning out perfectly crafted upholstery work.

He married, and bought a 1949 Mercury hard top. He customized it just like the ones he had seen from California, and soon a 1950 Mercury with an ohv V–8 followed. It was given the full treatment, with a diamond-pleated interior, shaved and decked bodywork, a perfect paint job and a hot motor.

Ermie was hearing rodding tales and reading every hot rodding publication that he could get his hands on. He lapped up the rodding world of the West Coast from his Phoenix home. Bonneville sounded fascinating. From a salvage yard, he rounded up a twenty-five-inch diameter T–33 belly tank, which was smaller than the P–38 tanks most racers were using to run on the salt flats. He searched the East Coast for parts and proceeded to build a streamliner for the 1956 Bonneville Speed Week. He fabricated a tube frame and built a 354–ci alcohol Hemi using Hilborn fuel injection.

The salt was in perfect condition that year, and in four runs, he set a new class record with a time of 217 mph, putting him in the 200 MPH Club.

He continued his auto upholstery business until 1956, but he was becoming increasingly well-known for his mechanical talent. His intense interest in going fast led to his carting a bunch of friends, including Jimmy Bryan, in the Mercury to the Indy 500. Bryan drove the famous "Van Dean Lines Special," and Ermie quickly gained a niche on the team as "a mechanic stooge," as he called the job, assisting Bob Christie and Clint Brawness. (Bryan started nineteenth and finished nineteenth in the 1956 Indy 500.)

This association with Indy developed over the next seven years, and in 1963, Ermie was the chief mechanic for the Van Dean Lines Special. He later became the chief mechanic on the "Spirit of St. Louis" team.

His fascination with, and commitment to, Bonneville also continued, and Ermie built a third streamliner during 1962 and 1963. It was powered by four Ford 427 big-block motors but, due to the wet weather in 1963, it didn't run. With another year to

Ermie (right) looks under the shell of the four-engined streamliner.

work out the bugs, Ermie rebuilt all the engines, opening them out to 500 ci apiece.

Unfortunately, 1963 could very well have been the end of the Immerso story. He was afflicted with a rare spinal cord tumor that immobilized and almost killed him. The tumor was benign, and a long and complex operation had him on the way to a 100 percent recovery. Not a man to be kept down for long, Ermie went back to work sixteen days later, tuning racing powerboats.

After his quick recovery, Ermie was hired at Carroll Shelby Racing in Venice, as the engine shop foreman. There he built and supervised the building of all Shelby's racing engines. It was a time of great success for them all. Shelby and his team of drivers were collecting many checkered flags in wins with Cobras, Mustangs, the King Cobra Can-Am car and the Daytona coupe.

In 1965, Ermie was restless and wanted to change jobs. Chuck Daigh at Holman-Moody in Long Beach offered him work building NASCAR-type engines for offshore powerboat racing. One of Ermie's jobs at Holman-Moody was to develop a new blown Ford 427 V–8 for offshore racing. This project proceeded well, with their motors winning the 1966 APBA West Coast Championships in Pete Rothchild's boat, "Thunderballs."

Seeing a new future before him, Ermie took the leap from regular employment and opened his own business, "Thunderbird Products." This business was begun to design and fabricate custom exhaust systems for race cars, but it didn't flourish. Ermie saw the error of his ways and switched to fabricating performance exhaust systems for street-driven cars.

The business did well, expanding to offer a complete line of aftermarket exhaust items, from low-restriction mufflers for VWs, to tuned-length headers for big-block Chevys.

Bonneville was still on Ermie's mind, but for the next twelve years, he did not race. He served twice as president of the 200 MPH Club and has continued to serve as a board member.

He converted the four-engined streamliner to turbine power with a Lycoming D–53 helicopter engine and readied it for a salt attempt in 1978. The streamliner turned on the works, running 265 mph, but aerodynamic instability limited its top speed.

At around this time, his interests were branching out. He wanted another street roadster and decided to build what he considered "the ideal traditional street roadster," not a fancy show car but a "hot-to-trot" roadster that could and would be driven.

The long process began in 1976. Using a Deuce roadster, the project that was to take just a few years eventually took a decade. It took him two tries to win the Oakland Roadster Show. In 1987, he was beaten out because he had proof-coated the underbody as part of his concept of building a fully drivable street roadster. So he took the roadster down to basics again and spent the year doing the entire underside in perfect gloss orange. Don "Buffy" Thelen of Buffalo Motor Cars had been instrumental in many facets of the roadster's fabrication and, again helped get the roadster one-hundred-point-perfect.

The aluminum-bodied Kraft Auto Special was ready to run at the Salt Flats when Ermie posed for this photo. The car was ready in 1963, but wet weather at the flats kept it from running. By the time Ermie brought it back, he had bored the four 427 engines out to 500 ci apiece.

In 1988 the roadster placed first in the esteemed Oakland show. Called "Orange Twist," the 1932 roadster was powered by a converted Ford flathead fitted with Ardun overhead valve conversion. It runs 284 ci and is fed off a six-pack of Stromberg 97s. The all-steel body is hung over a Kurtis Kraft-style tube axle.

Not a man to sit still, Ermie had another roadster in the works. This was a 1927 T that started off as an Oakland show car. With Ermie once again enlisting the help of Don Thelen, the original Oakland road-ster was built alongside the 1932 project. The '32 had started out to be a street driver but, as Ermie discov-ered, "hot rod projects just get out of hand." The '32 became an Oakland entry and eventual winner.

The 1927 Track T turned out to be a radical show car, with much gold plating, chrome, polished stainless steel and stunning detail, powered by a Ford twin overhead cam V–8 Indy race engine. It became the Oakland show's 1989 winner, taking the World's Most Beautiful Roadster prize and making Ermie a two-time winner, two years in a row.

Ermie seems to have boundless energy. While all the hot rod building was going on, he still found time to work on his new twin turbine-powered streamliner and finally built a street roadster. The dark blue beauty uses a 1929 Ford roadster body sitting on a 1932 frame with power from a flathead V–8. The streamliner is sure to cause a stir when it's finished. It uses a chromemoly tube frame that is custom-tailored around a pair of jet turbines. Ermie expected to have it on the salt in 1992. The body was designed by the brilliant Alex Tremulis.

Ermie Immerso wears a white chin beard and glasses that seems to perch on the end of his nose. His solid build and bib-and-braces give him a country

Ermie Immerso, circa 1990.

boy look, but behind his impish grin is a world of knowledge. He has followed a long and sometimes difficult path as he helped turn the daredevil sport of hot rodding into one of the most pleasurable occupa-tions known to mechanical-minded men.

This is a drawing of the four-engined, turbo-powered streamliner Ermie was working on in the early nineties, with hopes of having it ready to run in 1992.

Chapter 13

Ed Iskenderian

You wouldn't think a man would relish the fact that his life is a daily grind, but that's the way Ed Iskenderian loves it.

That's because high-tech grinding equipment helps him keep his title as the "Camfather," developer and manufacturer of the most important line of cams in racing over the years.

It's hard to imagine that Ed considers anything about his life to be a grind. He grew up in Los Angeles, the son of an Armenian shoemaker, and fell in love with hot rods early. He earned and learned his

way to the top of the automotive world because of his proficiency in developing cams to suit the exact needs of a variety of racers.

Today, he's a congenial hot rodding folk hero. Standing just under six feet tall, he sports a crew cut and has a familiar gap between his front teeth. Just as familiar is the huge, hand-rolled cigar he always seems to have close at hand, yet rare is the person who has ever seen him light it.

Ed posed proudly, cigar firmly between his teeth, in front of the factory on Broadway in Gardena, circa 1990.

Wearing a 1963 Bonneville Salt Flats T-shirt, Ed works on a Hemi dyno motor.

"Hi, pal," is his trademark greeting, and it's been heard by everyone from common street racers to racing's greatest drivers. Ed always has tech advice to offer, and can provide an instant performance evaluation of a V–8 engine based solely on a description of the motor's cam profile. His company's product catalog also offers lots of tech information, but the printed word can't present it in quite the same fashion as can the Camfather.

He was an early "gear head" as a teen, and loved any kind of automobile as long as it could go fast—preferably with him behind the wheel. In the thirties, Ed wanted his hot rods to be the fastest around but the go-goodies simply weren't easily available; their demand far outstripped the supply. The wait for manifolds, carbs and cams could be months. Even when the parts did arrive, they were not all they were cracked up to be. Ed thought that with the right equipment, he could build his own parts.

At Polytech High School in Los Angeles, Ed took every technical and automotive course available to get hands-on experience with cars, engine work, drafting and machining. His project at the college was to convert a Model T Ford truck into a hot rod roadster. Those days, it was possible to have a warmed-over roadster for less than $15.

Ed was among the earliest dedicated street racers. They would tear around the little towns that today make up the vast city of Los Angeles. The T was a flexible car and it got a solid beating in those early forays. Ed suffered repeated crankshaft fail-

ures, but there was a ready supply of cheap replacement engines in vacant lots in Los Angeles.

Ed earned his living and hot rod money specializing in Model T Fords, and through his dealings he found many special pieces of speed equipment. Always ready to try something new, Ed modified his Fords with overhead valve conversions and tried out Ford's A and B engines, but none were strong enough to endure the stress of street racing.

Ed remembered the early days of very little money but having big fun with cars when he and friends would gas up his Ford Model T and head out for a night of cruising and street racing:

Late one night Ed and a cruising buddy were racing home. As they screeched around a corner, their fuel tank (which was on the rear deck) toppled over and its contents poured out over the rear of the car, which burst into flames. Ed wheeled to a halt in the middle of an intersection, and they both abandoned ship. John raced away to find a hose, while Ed tried to dislodge the fuel tank.

John came racing back with a hose going flat out, but twenty feet from the Ford the hose stopped short, and the water pressure was too low to reach the car. Ed kicked at the car and managed to roll the tank off. Windows in neighboring houses lit up. The asphalt was now on fire and the boys decided it was time to depart. The sound of sirens in the distance hurried them. They managed to pull the car clear of the flames and doused the fire on the car with several bags. With the sirens getting louder, they pushed the

Ed used a shot of his famous 1927 Turtle-deck T as a holiday greeting card.

The famous Isky Clown dragster was used in a promotional shot at the San Fernando drags. It ran a Potvin blown small-block Chevy engine, but that didn't stop Ed from having some fun with it. Note the wind-up key sticking out of the tail of the car. Panorama City Kiwanis members posed with the car to promote a fund-raising race event.

Ford three blocks down the road and ran it into a driveway just as police cars arrived at the intersection. All they found was the road on fire and a Model T gas tank buried in the midst of the flames.

By the late-thirties, the first Ford V–8 had become easily available, and Ed turned his attention away from the T four-banger to the bent-eight. To his delight, he found that Ford had built a hot rodder's special with the new engine. The crank was stronger, with four times the bearing surface area, and it was counter-weighted. In its stock form, it could pull 85 mph on the dry lakes.

He built a lakester race car based on a Ford T frame, and exceeded 100 mph with the flathead Ford. Inventively, he worked the Ford over with a special "F" head that converted the flathead to a partial overhead valve. The intake valve remained in the block and the exhaust valve was converted to overhead valves. To this he added an Edelbrock slingshot manifold, and he modified the combustion chambers to increase the compression ratio. He filled the chambers by welding them up, and on the advice of Ed Winfield, recontoured the chambers to a 13:1 compression ratio. (This was an extremely high compression ratio even by today's standards, and the Ford was the fastest street hot rod in America at that time.)

Like all of us, Ed had a hero—and his was Ed Winfield. Winfield was a scientist and a car freak. He was the first of the cam grinders who really understood the technology of performance grinding of cams. When he was only eighteen, Ed decided that he should work with Winfield, even for no money, but his repeated offers were turned down.

To buy a cam from Winfield was an experience. He would not let anyone into his workshop; you had to stand in the street and talk to him through a six-inch gap in the door. But over the years, Ed gained Winfield's confidence and Winfield later helped Ed with his cam business.

Ed checked blueprints of a new design at the factory.

The war interrupted Ed's plans and put him to work in a factory in Long Beach, building aircraft for England. He worked as a tool and die maker, learning many skills that would help him later in his business. While working on aircraft at the Lockheed factory, he was also building and racing his car. He had money to spend but there was nothing to buy, and so he used his new machining skills to build his own performance parts.

In 1943, he was drafted into the U.S. Air Force. Hoping to become a fighter pilot, he went to flight school. But there were too many aspiring pilots, and instead, he became a tail gunner on a B–54. He was, in fact, the crew chief on military transport aircraft that flew from California to Australia and New Guinea. During the war, he spent a considerable amount of time in Australia and loved it, traveling all over the East Coast, chasing girls and drinking brown ale on the Queensland coast.

The war over, he returned to Los Angeles. By now, racers had money and they wanted to spend it. Dry lakes racing was at its height at Muroc Dry Lakes. (By the way, the name "Muroc" comes from the family who used to own a ranch that included the lake. Their name was "Corum," and Muroc is that name spelled backwards.)

Clay Smith was grinding his cams in Los Angeles, but there was still a three-month wait for a selected model. To Ed, this was the turning point. He wanted a performance cam but not at some time in the distant future. He knew how they were prepared, and he had the skills to grind his own, but he lacked the machinery.

He learned that he could buy a surplus cam grinder from the government for $3,500, but in those days, that was the price of a house, so he put his mind to work. He knew he could get a regular cylindrical grinding machine for a few hundred dollars, and with clever manipulation, he built his own cam grinder out of one of just such a common grinding machine.

He read everything he could find on cams and cam grinding, then built a special rocker bar mechanism for the cylindrical grinder and started grinding cams. His machine produced camshafts in their simplest form, and his cams gave a noticeable increase in performance over the factory racing cams.

The first few years were tough, but Iskenderian Racing Cams eventually prospered. Ed bought more grinders and slowly expanded his operations. His first shop was at the rear of Mercury Tool and Die in Culver City, today the site of Universal Studios. He built cams for street guys and racers alike, but a new challenge became his greatest interest. He built a series of special racing cams for the NASCAR circuit, but they were the best-kept speed secret of the circle racer using them; much to Ed's dismay, people didn't know they were running Isky Cams!

They were fast-acting cams that used a no-clearance ramp design and were excellent at giving stunning low-end acceleration. Ed had designed this cam after examining the Myer Drake Racing Cam, which used a radius tap profile.

With the invention of the cam copy grinder for making cam masters, the cam industry suddenly became wide open to anyone. Ed survived this period of turmoil and saw many businesses come and go. His biggest gripe even today is the low quality of cams sold by cam "repackagers" who don't own their own grinding equipment. He says customers buy Isky cams after they have tried other cams. One cheap cam that Ed checked was given to him because it had produced excessive valve train noise. He found that the cam had flaws in the cam lobes and closing ramps—flaws that were visible to the naked eye. There was also a large variation in the taper of each lobe, a critical factor in determining lifter and cam life, and it was obviously affecting the engine's performance.

Through the years, Ed's help and development work has benefited many American racers as well as the giant manufacturers. Ed has researched cams for Ford, Jaguar and Nissan. The smaller, more exotic

The famous CamFather decal with the caricature of Ed with his big cigar and a cam under his arm.

The components of a complete Isky high-performance valvetrain are laid out.

manufacturers such as Ferrari, Lamborghini and Maserati have also sought Ed's technology to help their performance.

Ed was the first of the cam grinders to move with the times when the great oil embargo struck in 1973. He developed special economical cams which gave better low-end torque and improved fuel

Ed Iskenderian pauses to reflect at his shop in Gardena, California, circa 1990.

economy. They were called the Mile-a-More and were designed to be suitable for all V–8s. Special grinds were made available for high-performance applications.

Today, Iskenderian Racing Cams is run by two of Ed's sons, Richard and Ronald, who handle the everyday affairs of the company while Ed develops ideas for varied automotive applications and works on industrial machinery business. He also often stays at a small coastal village in Baja, where he partakes in one of his other loves: fishing.

Ed has not only produced a huge variety of cams but has also developed a range of engine valve train components and special tools. Ed's inventive nature has produced many new ideas and products.

The self-guiding roller tappet is one of his inventions. It requires no machining to install and its self-locking design bridges the matched pair of roller tappets, allowing for easy slip-in installation. The roller tappet has some important advantages over the conventional flat design; it reduces frictional drag, practically eliminating cam wear, and helps lower engine oil temperature. The roller tappet also allows for higher potential with its inherently higher spring loads, which overcome forces of inertia and maintain valve gear stability. Also, with high-lift cams, the rate of valve lift per degree is not limited to the available tappet diameter, as with a flat tappet camshaft.

Another of Ed's special trick ideas is the Groov-o-matic, a hand-driven tool for O-ring cylinders, which helps prevent blown head gaskets in supercharged, turbocharged and high-compression engines.

Ed has always had a flamboyant approach to his work. His "Camfather" advertising series and his full-page cartoon series about the cam industry were cited as one of the best performance industry ad campaigns of the seventies.

The world's largest manufacturer of racing cams, Iskenderian Racing Cams still maintains a large factory in Gardena, California. There, Norton cam grinders grind all Iskenderian cams, and the back building is a dyno facility used for constant testing of camshaft and valve train components.

Isky buys and tests most new engines produced by the major manufacturers for valve gear. A second dyno is used for endurance testing of racing engines, and the results are available to all engine builders, whether professionals or at-home builders. The information is dispensed in the form of horsepower charts, and data on carburetion, jetting, ignition and timing is included in the company's catalog.

From a humble beginning as the son of an Armenian shoemaker, Ed Iskenderian has a business that reaches around the world, and his logo, an orange circle with a large capital "I" in the center, represents the ultimate in quality cams and engine components.

Chapter 14

Tommy Ivo

It's not often that a discussion of drag racing's great drivers crosses paths with the "Trivial Pursuit" question, "Who were the stars of the 'My Little Margie' TV show?" but it has happened.

That's because when the discussion turns to drag racing's great early professionals, the name Tommy Ivo is bound to come up. Known as the sport's first full-time professional driver, Tommy made a name for himself worldwide with his driving and with his gorgeous cars. But before he gained his fame on the drag strips, he was already well-known in the enter-

tainment world, where he had been performing since he was just learning to walk.

Tommy was born in Denver in 1936, and his mother had him tap dancing at the same time he was learning to walk. He enjoyed great success in local talent shows, but because the mountain climate caused his mother's arthritis to flare up, the family moved to Burbank, California.

Tommy got involved in show biz in southern California, and was a regular on the "Vanities" show at the Earl Carrol Theater in Hollywood at age

The famous four-Buick-engined Tommy Ivo "Showboat" dragster at the San Diego Drags.

Seven years old and already a seasoned performer, Tommy was setting the stage for the next thirty years as a national celebrity.

seven. A producer picked him out of the cast for a film role, and his screen career was launched. He performed in more than 100 movies including: "Rebel Without a Cause," "Tarzan" and "I Remember Mama."

As television grew in the forties, so did Tommy's career, which led to his starring in several TV roles. "It was hard to believe that I was being paid for playing," Tommy recalled of those days.

He was in more than 200 TV shows, including "The Mickey Mouse Club," "The Donna Reed Show" and "My Little Margie." He worked with many of Hollywood's great talents, including William Holden and Boris Karlov.

By the time he was sixteen, Tommy had built up a good nest egg from his show business paychecks, and he bought a new 1954 Buick Roadmaster. It was a two-door hardtop that didn't remain stock for long. No, Tommy jumped on the customizing trend of the day and shaved the door handles and frenched the headlights.

He continued to work in TV and films, but he was still considered a "child actor," which meant his daily work hours were limited so he could continue his school work. That left him with plenty of spare time, some of which he filled by taking part in local street racing, but he was looking for something more interesting.

At about this time, he rode with a friend one Saturday down to the Santa Ana Drags to see the hot rodders run on the quarter-mile. On his second visit Tommy was racing the Buick. The car's weakest point, its Dynaflow transmission, had Tommy

Tommy was a consistent winner, but the NHRA inspectors kept bugging him about his racer's safety and appearance. Tommy built this wild beast in a week and took it racing, *much to the dismay of the inspectors, who could not fault it on safety requirements.*

In 1960, a young Tommy at the wheel of his famous twin Buick-engined dragster ran 180 mph in less than nine seconds.

Tommy in 1967. "The ace of the front wheel flyers" blasts down the strip, blazing the rear tires in one of his Ivo-built fuel cars.

The remains of one of Tommy's rear-engined fuel cars after a crash at Pomona.

stumped. It needed constant attention and rebuilding, but he managed to win his class track record with the car.

After a few months of throwing the Buick down the quarter-mile, Tommy saw Norm Grabowski's roadster on a cruise. It was sitting in a slot at Bob's Big Boy in Glendale and was the wildest-looking roadster he had ever seen. He knew he had to have one. Using an A frame, a 1955 Buick V–8 and a 1925 T with a shortened pickup bed, Tommy built a roadster and quickly became Santa Ana's undefeated champ.

Having cleaned up on the field of local racers, Tommy went looking for more action; dragsters seemed like the logical step. Tommy commissioned Kent Fuller to build a one-hundred-inch dragster chassis, and he had a body made of hand-formed aluminum for the staggering 1955 price of $125; the total cost of the car was $500.

The dragster became a state-of-the-art racer. It was initially powered by a single, fuel-injected, ethyl-burning Buick engine. It ran hard, but the showman in Tommy got him thinking about converting the dragster to a two-engine configuration.

1960 was a year of change and challenge as Tommy saw the potential to become the first touring professional drag racer. He changed the dragster's configuration to twin-engine setup and went east on his first professional tour. His assistant on that tour was young Don Prudhomme.

The twin-motored digger was set up using a pair of Buicks mated together by meshing the ring gears. One engine ran backwards and used a special reverse-billet cam that Ed Iskenderian had ground for the motor. They were fed by Hilborn fuel injection and produced around 450 hp apiece.

Tommy with his alloy-bodied fuel car in 1967.

Tommy and Don Prudhomme in an exhibition match. N. Blake

"The crowds back East loved the car and the whole scene appealed to my sense of showmanship. I also figured that if two engines got that much reaction, then four engines should really blow them away," recalled Tommy.

Back on the West Coast after the tour, Tommy began work on one of the most famous dragsters of all time: "Showboat." He was still a regular on the "Margie" show, but when the car appeared on the cover of *Hot Rod* magazine, the producers of the show nearly had a fit. They had figured Tommy was just out tooling about in a little weekend stocker, but a fire-breathing, tire-smoking, four-engined dragster was a different matter. Twentieth Century Fox officials freaked out at what they saw as Tommy's dangerous weekend activities. But "TV Tommy" had had enough of "lights, camera, action." He wanted his light to run red, orange and green.

Tommy on tour as one of the first professional drag racers. His custom-built Dodge truck carried two dragsters and his Corvette on top.

Tommy hired several drivers to run the car while he finished his contract on the TV show. His eastern tour the previous year had shown him he could make as much money racing cars as he could acting. Tommy wiped the slate clean and became a full-time professional drag racer.

Showboat became the first financially successful drag racing exhibition car, and Tommy Ivo became one of the "golden gods of drag racing." He toured the entire country, then went to England and the rest of Europe, doing his crowd-pleasing, tire-burning exhibition runs.

Showboat was built quite quickly. It used two pairs of fuel-injected Buick motors that were offset, with one pair driving the rear wheels and the other pair driving the fronts. The front drive used an Indy Novi front-wheel drive assembly. It also proved to be a most dependable car, as it ran more than fifteen years with not much more than a new set of front tires. The NHRA banned four-engine cars but let Tommy use Showboat as a crowd draw for events. Eventually, Showboat was sold and modified to become the "Wagon Master."

Tommy moved on to new classes, opening his own chassis shop to build and maintain his fleet of cars. In 1962, he built his first fuel car covered with a perfect Bob Sorrell aluminum body. It was powered by a blown Hemi and was the first car to run in the 190–mph zone. Tommy toured England and re-

Tommy grins for the photographers in 1966.

membered with delight how he dusted Don Garlits.

Tommy was, by now, locked into full-time professional match racing and in 1964 he raced against Garlits fifty-two times, a record in anyone's books. During the next ten years, Tommy continued to race everywhere, building more than twenty-five new cars. During this time, he became the first man into the seven-second zone with a single-engine car.

Tommy went on the road in 1968 with a matched pair of AA/Fuel dragsters, crossing the country in a glass-sided Dodge truck. A red Corvette was carried on top for local transportation at events. Tommy's showmanship shone through, enhancing his image. He became a proponent of fire burnouts. His amazing flaming departures into "the traps" were alway front-page stuff but in the mid-seventies there was a decline in interest in Top Fuel racing, so Tommy moved on, to build his first Funny Car.

In 1976 he ran a Dodge Aspen for the Rod Shop, but the economic demands from trying to keep an expensive car alive and also make a living were too great. Not wanting to sit on the sidelines and watch, Tommy moved into jet cars which would let him give spectators the thrills and the show he was renowned for. Fire burnouts were legal, and he delighted in doing exhibition runs.

By this time in his career, he had picked up a wild collection of nicknames: TV Tommy, Poison Ivo, Instant Ivo, Pyro Ivo. He has cherished these names over the years and still owns his collection of original helmets bearing these appropriate titles.

Jet cars were a big part of his life in the late-seventies, but his intense interest in drag racing waned. He felt too restricted by new regulations and safety requirements, and the demands of building, running a team and racing were wearing him thin.

Sponsorship was harder to get and Tommy could see the writing on the wall. He predicted, just like Tony Nancy, that by the late-eighties, there would be about ten top teams and a handful of also-rans. And, like Nancy, he had no intention of being an also-ran. The days of everyone having the same equipment were gone and virtually overnight, multi-million dollar race teams had taken their place.

Tommy had done it all. He match-raced around the world; drove thousands of exhibition runs; participated in every major series in drag racing; and had come within a hair's breadth of winning the national finals.

By the early-eighties, Tommy was out of racing, taking a break. He had things to do at home that were neglected in his thirty years on the road. He started on an extensive home project, and one afternoon went out to pick up some bricks. Ten blocks from his home, he took a wrong turn. Driving down an alley to turn around, he spotted an old drag car trailer. Amazingly, he recognized it as the trailer that had been used to haul the "Wagon Master." A tingle ran down his spine, but he had more pressing needs: to get his bricks. Tommy didn't know whether the car was inside the trailer; he had sold Showboat to Tom McCourry more than twenty years ago. McCourry had converted Showboat into the Riviera Wagon Master, and Tom had not seen it in fifteen years.

That night, the idea of owning the old, four-engined car again started to play on him, and the next morning, Tommy returned for a closer inspection. Yes, the car was inside the trailer, but the owner didn't seem interested in selling it. The car had been in the trailer for fifteen years. Its tires were flat, the engines were frozen and everything else was a disaster. Tommy upped the buying price until finally the owner agreed to sell.

A long period of restoration ensued, but finally, after every part of the car was renewed, refreshed or replated, Tommy was back in the exhibition business. He spent a year on the road doing an exhibition tour.

In May of 1982 at the Saskatoon raceway, "Wagon Master" hit a frost wave in the track surface.

The wave had presented no problem during his warm-up runs, but during the exhibition run, Wagon Master slammed across it with so much force that it damaged three vertebrae in Tommy's back. It was time to call it quits.

Tommy was laid up for a long period of recuperation and the Wagon Master was again retired. It was sent to the Garlits Museum in Florida to take its place among the most famous drag racing cars of all time.

Tommy is back working on his home and various business ventures. He still looks fifteen years younger than he actually is, and his refreshing brightness is still very apparent.

In the blink of an eye, Tommy Ivo made the transition from being a star of the silver screen and TV screen to the star of the quarter-mile. His showmanship and stunning race cars always set the standard for others to follow. He was a pioneering champion in the sport of professional drag racing.

Tommy with Frankie Avalon in 1966 on the set of "Bikini Beach Party."

Chapter 15

Dean Jeffries

"Hollywood" will forever be a word capable of conjuring up images of glamorous stars, newsmaking events, amazing stunts and fantastic cars.

Those are images that have drawn millions to the show business capital over the years, and they were certainly images that appealed to Dean Jeffries.

Dean was born in Compton, California, where his father was a mechanic. Dean loved cars and helped his father work on them when he was young, but he made up his mind that a lifetime of oil stains and dirty hands was not very appealing.

Dean drove a 1932 Chevy coupe to Compton High School, and about that time he developed an interest in paint and panel work. He honed his skills as a teen, and traded his coupe and a 1939 Plymouth for a 1948 Mercury Coupe to satisfy his urge to run with the hot rod crowd.

Many a Friday night was spent cruising, drag racing on the divided freeway leading to Long Beach and pulling through the lot at Harvey's Drive-In. Dean would do a "cruiser's pass" through the lot, and the inevitable exchanges between drivers would lead to challenge races, many of which left Dean a few dollars richer.

These were the days when Pete Peterson was selling his two-page *Hot Rod* magazine for a nickel at the drag meets, and it was the same time that Dean went to work at the Compton Custom Shop owned by George Cernie. He learned the art of pinstriping and met the legendary Von Dutch, master of pinstriping. As pinstriping became more popular, Dean's services were in great demand. He opened his own shop on Atlantic Boulevard in Compton to do custom paint, panel work and pinstriping. Compton was one of the birthplaces of hot rodding. In the area, Ed Iskenderian was grinding cams, Ed

Roth was building, painting and striping cars, and Von Dutch was working and teaching his magic.

Dean's customers came from all over the United States. He had a booming business, but was dissatisfied with merely working as a pinstriper. He knew he had a greater calling in his work with cars, but just what it was, he didn't know.

At around this time, he was doing custom car work for some Hollywood stars. He recalled, "One afternoon, a good-looking young guy pulls up in a Porsche Spyder Speedster and wanders into my workshop. It was James Dean. He'd heard I was hot and he wanted some touches to highlight his silver racer."

In 1958, he acquired a Porsche Carrera and gave it a classic Californian custom job. His rodder friends liked the conversion, but Porsche owners were not impressed. He had tricked up the body and sprayed the Carrera Candy Pearl Silver.

Starting in the early-sixties, May became a time for Dean to be in Indianapolis for the 500. His love of race cars led him to visit one year and rent a booth in Gasoline Alley. What he learned from the race car builders about frame and sheet metal fabrication gave him the technology to become a proficient specialty body builder.

During his yearly visits to Indy, his fame grew among the race car owners, and one year, he was responsible for paint and artwork on twenty-two of the race cars. He would go to Indy alone and work eighteen to twenty hours a day on his custom paint jobs using exotic colors and combinations. A. J. Foyt was one of his early customers and they remain great buddies. One of Dean's toys is one of Foyt's Camaro racers, which he hopes to put back on the street for some fun.

Dean continued to do custom building and

general body work, and he was invited to enter the Oakland Tournament of Fame for the best hot rod. Using an early Maserati race car frame and running gear, he styled "Manta Ray," a low, sleek, single-seater race car hot rod. It had a remote-control starter, other remote control features and a lift top.

His first attempt at the radio control setup worked well until someone turned on a radio transmitter nearby. Suddenly, the Manta Ray started itself in the workshop, freaking out Dean and the workshop crew. A heavyweight remote control system quickly rectified the problem.

The car was tube-framed with an alloy skin covering the frame, race car-style. A single headlight was centered in the long twin-point nose. It was powered by a 289 Ford and was originally fitted with down-draft Webers, but Dean replaced them with a four-barrel Holley in the early seventies. Dean is a perfectionist, and the internal work was as stunning as the body. He machine-finished the alloy tanks and fittings before covering them with the skin.

The Manta Ray was the first show car to use braided lines. In the sixties, it was possible to go into

The Oakland Roadster Show-winning "Manta Ray." This view shows off its asymmetrical styling.

a surplus store and buy boxes of assorted braided hoses for $5. Dean used these for every fluid-carrying application on the Manta Ray, and it was one of the finishing touches that helped him win the coveted Oakland trophy. He formed the bubble roof

Dean with his current hot rod, a chopped 1934 Ford with outrageous flames.

A top view of the "Manta Ray."

using a vacuum process (which was different from the air-blown technique Ed Roth used to form his bubble on "Beatnik Bandit"). The vacuum process produces no distortion in the acrylic when it is

The "Monkeemobile" built for the TV show "The Monkees." It was based on a 1966 Pontiac GTO.

formed. Dean still owns the Manta Ray and it is the centerpiece in his showroom.

This project and the 1964 Oakland trophy opened many doors for Dean. He began customizing far more and doing less routine body work. Since he was the heart of the world's top movie studios, Dean had a superb opportunity to build specialty cars for the film industry. "Work," for Dean, means sixteen-hour days, six days a week. When building a car for a movie project, one day past a deadline can mean thousands of dollars lost, so Dean was always aware of the need to get a job done on time.

One of his first major movie cars was the "Monkeemobile" for the TV show "The Monkees." It was based on a 1966 Pontiac GTO. The car was used in the opening scene and occasionally during the show, but never saw much more action. (AMT, the model maker, made a model of it in ⅟₃₂nd scale.) The car was extensively modified, with the roof cut away, the trunk removed, the nose extended and a twenties-style phaeton touring top. It had the look of a drag racer, with a blower sticking out of the hood, wild exhaust headers protruding from the front wheelwells and a parachute that really worked styled into the tail.

Dean also built a tow-along trailer that unfolded for a portable stage, in case the band wanted to have an instant rock concert on the side of the freeway. The car was well built and has stood the test of time; it still is used regularly in music videos.

In 1966, Dean was commissioned to build a car for the TV series "The Green Hornet." This specialty car was based on the 1966 Chrysler Imperial four-door hardtop. It had a cannon mounted in the grille and a pair of rocket launchers fitted below each headlight. The body was modified with a completely new front end and special custom rear. The car was finished in gloss black with lime-green trim.

By this time, Dean was not only building cars for the movies, he was also doing both motorcycle and car stunts and progressed to rigging cars and building camera mounts for action scenes. In the Charles Bronson movie "Mr. Majestic," he set up a big sedan with a cannon that fired and flipped the car. The cannon was a mortar-like device, weighing around 400 pounds and mounted into the floor of the vehicle beside the driver. It was loaded with six to twelve ounces of quick-flash dynamite powder and its firing had to be timed precisely so the cameras could catch the action.

His movie vehicle business expanded as his reputation grew, and he built the Moon Buggy for the James Bond film "Diamonds Are Forever." It was an oddball, his first futuristic vehicle. It was originally going to have only a small part and be mostly non-functional, but in the final presentation, it climbed out of a crater, jumped off a cliff, and drove through extremely rough terrain at speeds up to 110 kph. The

Dean built the "Lunar Rover" for several James Bond movies.

Dean built the "Land Rover" for the movie "Damnation Alley" in record time. It performed without fault, confirming Dean's status as king of the movie car business.

retrieving arms were functional but were never used in the movie.

Some of Dean's vehicles have been totally destroyed in films. In "Death Race 2000," his cars were crashed, blown up and burned. They had weird names, too. The "Roman Lion" was based on a Fiat, the "Calamity Jane" was a Corvair, and the "Gangster Machine Gun," "Frankenstein Alligator" and "Herman the German V–1 Buzz Bomb" were all based on Volkswagens.

Dean found that VWs were excellent for his style of movie vehicles. They have a solid platform, the engine profile is low and self-contained (being air-cooled) and the automatic transmissions (which are tricked up by B&M) make them easy for actors to drive.

He has more than forty movies to his credit, for stunts or custom cars, and he has often provided both for a movie. He is a member of the Hollywood Screen Actors Guild and is considered one of Hollywood's top stuntmen.

Today, Dean is Hollywood's car genius and he still builds super-freaky movie cars. He built a VW-based exotic called "The Coyote," which looked like

Dean Jefferies drives a Ford Bronco in a stunt he performed for the film "Romancing the Stone."

a mixture of Lamborghini, aircraft and space module. This super silver sports car was used in movie and television shows, including the TV pilot "High Performance," for TV's "Fall Guy" and in the movie "Other Worlds." This futuristic road racer is fully functional. Its frame was built up with half-inch box tube and the body was hammered out of twenty-two-gauge sheet steel. It has Gullwing doors, and the interior has a sports car look. The car is powered by a VW engine producing more than 140 hp and hooking up to a B&M-prepared VW automatic transmission that has been reworked with heavier clutch bands, a 2500-rpm stall converter and an external oil cooler.

With such attention to detail, it's easy to see why Dean's car-building services are sought so often. Like his other cars, the Coyote is reliable and fast. It has a fully controllable suspension which allows the car to be set according to needs.

After the car was sold to another stuntman for his personal transportation, Dean just smiled when asked if he would be sad to see it go. "God no, I can build another of those babies in five weeks," he laughed.

His driving is also top-notch. For the movie "Honky Tonk Freeway," Dean was required to coordinate a stunt involving a motorhome, a truck full of oranges, ten cars, one limo, one Thunderbird coupe, one Excaliber and ten other scenery cars. To cap this off, Dean was to drive a five-ton truck with a rhinocerous in the back through this group of cars while they all crashed, and then jump a blown-up freeway bridge. He drove the stunt without the rhino and sailed the truck more than eighty feet before crashing down on the freeway on the other side of the non-existent bridge. The stunt injured him slightly, but he was soon right back to work.

Dean has a pleasant California way about him. His six-foot frame tells you he is strong and able. His mop of greying hair tells you he is over forty.

His office is a cluttered assortment of projects past, present and future. The showroom walls that surround the Manta Ray are covered with photos of his cars and movie stunts. On his desk are illustrations for a giant killer truck for a new movie project, a low-level VW sports car and parts for his GT 40

Dean worked as the lead stunt man on "Honky Tonk Freeway." In this scene, he jumped a GMC truck over an open freeway bridge, breaking his back upon landing.

roadster. Dean sits at his drawing board to brainstorm ideas. It was at that board that he dreamed up the "Landmaster" from "Damnation Alley," the most difficult project he has undertaken. He was given the script, then worked with the movie company's art department and the producer to come up with a design to meet all the script's needs and still be totally different from anything previously seen on the screen. That's what creative genius is all about.

Dean's first love is his cars, and his workshop displays his perfectionist nature; it is clean, organized and well-lit, and each project has its own area. His personal cars are extremely well preserved: a Mercedes 450 coupe, the Foyt Camaro racer, and the only remaining Ford GT-40 roadster in the world. He also has a stunning 1934 Ford Hot Rod that has been chopped, channeled and sectioned; it is white with an outstanding flame job running wildly all over its front.

It's said that in every genius there is a little madness. If that is true, it's not hard to see why Dean Jeffries is still car-crazy after all these years.

Chapter 16

Robert "Jocko" Johnson

Robert "Jocko" Johnson was destined to live in the fast lane, but with him, the man known to produce some of the fastest "works of art" in the drag racing world, that road would likely be twisty as well as fast.

Jocko was reputedly a direct descendent of thirteen kings of England, yet he was a California kid whose fast lane was not lined with kings and coronets, but, rather, with modified roadsters, coupes, the dry lakes and Bonneville.

Jocko got a lot of his automotive inspiration from his older brother Don and the photos Don would bring home from trips to the races at El Mirage dry lakes. The photos fascinated Jocko, and instilled a love of cars in his young mind.

Across the street lived Dean Brown, the starter at both the Fontana and Irwindale raceways. Jocko remembered the first races he went to with his brother and Brown. He was about ten years old, and the races were at the Fontana airport. The cars were tiny, gas-powered midget racers which ran on a line around a central pole; it didn't matter much what they were, they were race cars and Jocko was stoked!

At Lynnwood High School, many students had modified roadsters and Jocko joined the group with his own 1932. One afternoon, "his ship came in" because a buddy wanted a lift to his after-school job at Barris Customs. Jocko couldn't believe his ears: "You've got a job at the Barris shop? Let's roll!"

The Allison-powered "Jocko Liner" under testing, with the engine exposed. This vehicle would become the "Moon Liner."

Jocko had seen the Barris Brothers shop mentioned in the hot rod magazines and was eager to see it.

In no time, Jocko landed a job at Barris, working for $1 an hour. George Barris taught him how to fold sandpaper and sand sheet metal. Jocko soon became Barris's favorite paint prep man. But it was Sam, George's creative brother, who became Jocko's mentor.

Sam was the art behind the Barris shop. George would draw the cars and promote them, Sam and the Manoke brothers, John and Ralph, built them, and "Junior" painted them. Today Junior is the owner of "Junior's House of Color" and is the most famous automotive paint man in the world.

Sam and the Manoke brothers were a terrific team, with Sam as the master metal shaper and the Manoke brothers as the lead artists. These older metal craftsmen let Jocko watch over their shoulders as they performed their metal miracles. No other place on earth could have provided such a perfect environment for this young and creative mind, who was bent on shaping slick sheet metal to wrap it around fast cars. "I would stand around for hours just watching these guys turn Detroit iron into custom cars," he recalled.

Chet Herbert contracted with George Barris to build him a streamliner body. Rod Shapel designed the body and ran it through a wind tunnel. Once they agreed on the final shape, George gave Jocko the loft lines to glue to plywood and then cut out the shapes so that they could be made into a buck for the sheet metal formers.

This experience gave Jocko a superb overview of the process of how streamliner bodies were fabricated. Jocko was used to taking an existing car and modifying it; building the streamliner was the entirely new process of developing a car from an idea.

Its performance was surprising. At Bonneville, it set eleven international records with its unblown fuel 331 Chrysler. Its top speed was 245 mph, with Leeroy Niemeyer driving. Niemeyer claimed the streamliner handled so well that he could "read the funny pages" running at 240 mph.

Jocko was fascinated. He wanted more speed and better cars and wanted to design his own, but he didn't know how to start. He became a student of the European school of race car design and studied streamliner ideas and aerodynamics. Such streamliners as John Cobbs' "Railton" and Malcolm Campbell's "Bluebird" would become catalysts for Jocko's streamliner ideas.

By this time, George had tagged Robert as "Jocko." Robert had been working on a project and was scratching as most guys do at some time. George noticed this and shouted, "Hey, jock itch, get over here." The guys around the shop all fell over laughing and overnight Robert became "Jocko."

Jocko didn't stay with the Barris brothers much longer. In 1954, he moved back to Lakewood to

Streamliner number two in Chet Herbert's livery.

work for Scotty Fenn at Experimental Automotive. Jocko learned the art of the die grinder, and he developed his skills modifying hundreds of flatheads under Fenn's watchful eye. He also got the feel for what would and would not work on ohc heads. According to Jocko, Fenn told him to think like a molecule of air racing down the port: "You want the smoothest, quickest way through that hole."

Around the corner was Lakewood Muffler. The crew there ran Mickey Thompson's streamlined dragster with an Ardun on board and occasionally ran it up and down Artesia Boulevard just for fun. The roar of the Ardun hurling itself past the shop attracted Jocko like a moth to a nightlight. He soon made friends with the crew at Lakewood Muffler and started helping with race cars at their shop.

It was this connection that helped him start the famous "Jocko's Porting Service" in a small bay at Lakewood Muffler's hot rod shop. Jocko made a deal with Gary Cagle, the owner of the shop. Jocko would help maintain the cars and keep the workshop clean and tidy in return for use of part of the shop for his porting service.

It didn't take long for the business to develop. The talents he had learned at Experimental Automo-

The famed accident when the laws of physics gave Jocko an irrefutable demonstration of down-force versus insufficient substructure. The body tore off the streamliner during this run with Jazzy Nelson driving.

The streamlined fuel dragster sponsored by Clay Smith Cams used a body built by Jocko.

The first drag racing airfoil was a Jocko wing on Lee Pendleton's V-12 Allison-powered dragster. Jocko suggested to Lee that he could achieve more downforce with an inverted wing. It worked out perfectly and Don Garlits followed with his own version several weeks later.

tive, building hot rod flatheads, were put to good use. Jocko placed a few $7.50 ads in the drag racing newspapers and then went on the road to get business from the Los Angeles area speed shops. They were obviously impressed with the products he showed and he soon had more work than he could handle. Jocko took over the lease of the old Lakewood Muffler hot rod workshop and there, on South Street in North Long Beach, Jocko built the first of his streamliners.

The first Jocko's Porting Service streamliner was in perfect form. The design produced so much down force, however, that it tore the front section clean off the frame during its first hard run. Jazzy

Nelson was driving the 450-ci Cagle Hemi-powered car when it disintegrated. Cagle and Jocko had used a special chromemoly frame and powered it with one of the first top-mounted blown Hemis.

It took awhile to figure out why the streamliner had broken, but Jocko got to work building another alloy-bodied car powered by an Allison V-12. Pieces of the wrecked streamliner's chassis were used to build the new car.

Building streamliners was a side business, but it did develop a few interesting twists. Jocko had the reputation as an innovator, and when Lee Pendleton saw the ideas that he was trying to incorporate into his streamliners, he asked him what he could do for his dragster, which needed a vast increase in down force to stop the Allison V-12 from smoking the tires the whole way down the track.

Alterations had to be kept simple because Pendleton didn't have much money. So Jocko attached a

The chassis for the first fiberglass "Jocko Liner," without its engine.

pair of inverted airfoils to the front section of the dragster body, giving it the down force it needed to "glue it to the ground." Don Garlits saw the idea, liked it and installed a pair on his "Swamp Rat."

The early-sixties were a time of innovation, and it seemed that everyone wanted porting services. Jocko was one of only two reliable porting men in Los Angeles, and as he studied the work of British engine builder Harry Westlake, his application of Westlake's theory worked with great results.

In 1967, Jocko began preparing drag racing heads for Keith Black. Black was a Chrysler engine builder and Chrysler decided to go Trans-Am racing. They wanted a man to do the heads for the down-sized 340 V–8. Chrysler liked what Jocko offered and contracted with him to develop a set of Trans-Am heads for the motor. He went home and carved out the ports, moving them one-and-one-half inches up the heads. On the dyno, the engine turned an extra 44 hp, 50% better than any other porting service.

Chrysler was delighted with Jocko's work. He suggested that they could easily achieve the same result, which would be much stronger, if they would simply change the core boxes at the foundry when they cast the heads. They did this for a run of racing heads that went to Jocko for porting and polishing. Sam Posey, driving the Dodge Trans-Am, did well with the Jocko Hemi heads that year but was beaten by Parnelli Jones in a Ford.

By the mid-seventies, Jocko had tired of engine building and wanted some new direction in his life. He used his background in carving heads to begin carving wood sculptures and other art. He also moved to Twenty-Nine Palms to get away from the city.

His first wife did not like desert life and moved back to Laguna Beach; Jocko moved to Florida for six months to help Garlits build his black streamliner. Florida did not agree with Jocko and after six months, he moved back to California, renting a house with his son Ben in Capistrano Beach.

Dean Moon with the "Moon Liner" at Bonneville. Dean later converted it to a V–8–powered drag racer and TV appearance car.

Jocko with one of his exotic wood sculptures. He worked as a professional artist for many years after building the "Jocko Liners," and later returned to work on his automotive interests.

Across the road lived a family with three daughters. The youngest one became a playmate of Ben's and Jocko married the oldest, who also had a great affection for Twenty-Nine Palms. Her family had homesteaded a tract of land there forty years earlier, and she had spent most of her summers in the desert. It was a great match—not only two artists but two people who liked the desert life; they bought a place with two houses and a shop.

Jocko worked seriously as a professional sculptor and furniture builder for the next ten years, but the art world and its cliquish nature did not agree with him in the least. "Standing around at an art show opening, wearing a suit and tie and trying to look intelligent with a bunch of folks who had no idea of what you were trying to do, was not my kind of fun," he recalled. Jocko enjoyed the physical side of the profession, however. He created many fine pieces, and even placed in a prestigious California Design Show.

Jocko quit the art scene and got back into automobiles. Ferrari and early hot rod restorations became the "fare of the day."

Jocko and son Ben are co-workers these days. Their personal project is the "Triple Nickel," a 555–mph streamliner that should cover the measured mile in 6.3 seconds. A launch vehicle will tow this three-engined streamliner to 180 mph before "launching" it down the salt.

It's not so much the speed record that Jocko wants, but, rather, the space and time to prove a few of his theories. As he has said before, "It's a matter of trying that counts. If you don't make a go of what you believe in, then your idea is not worth a damn."

Jocko in front of "Triple Nickel."

Chapter 17

Dick Landy

Dick Landy was born some fifty-plus years ago in Van Nuys, California, the son of an immigrant farmer whose family was staking out a new life for itself in California. The family lived on a small farm in Grenada Hills, where at an early age, Dick learned to drive the family tractor. (His love of the land and the region never failed him; he still lives close to where he was reared.)

Unlike so many teenagers of the day, Dick wasn't particularly interested in cars when he was in high school. He was preoccupied earning All-Southern California honors as a star tackle on the football team at Valley High and Notre Dame High in San Fernando. Still, he had a set of wheels, a 1940 Chevy coupe, that he drove to and from school and used to cruise with his sweetheart (who became his wife and main "teammate" for the past thirty-plus years) Jean Beahrs.

Eventually, the budding hot rod craze in southern California caught Dick's attention. He and Voleten Goely, a good buddy, built a street and track racer out of Goely's 1953 Ford coupe. They dropped in a 1954 Ford's 246-ci ohv V-8 and the car really flew, giving Dick his first taste of speed on wheels. At the dry lakes they made a run of 119 mph, not bad for a couple guys making their first run with an old Ford that was still Goely's daily driver.

Their success at the lakes encouraged them to pursue more excitement at the drags. Running the '53 with a few more modifications, Dick and Goely got one class record but learned that the cast-iron flywheel on the Ford blew apart at around 6000 rpm.

Dick's next automotive adventure was with Vince Hart and a 1956 Ford pickup, for which he became both mechanic and driver. In the mid-fifties, the drags offered a special class for pickups, and it became a major division at most California strips. Dick and Hart ran the 270 V-8-powered Ford at the

Long Beach, Saugas and San Fernando strips, where they dominated the class with 92-mph passes. Dick did most of the driving since Vince couldn't get a handle on power-shifting the three-on-the-tree column shifter. Dick remembered, "We won a heck of a lot of races, which pleased Vince. There was no

Rugged good looks, plenty of driving talent and an outgoing, friendly personality made Dick a big crowd pleaser both on and off the track.

Dick's first Ford factory car was the Andy Andrews-sponsored 1962 406 tri-power, two-door lightweight.

money to be had in prizes, but we always came away with a trophy and a pass for the following week's races."

During the next few years, Dick left drag racing altogether, but he didn't leave the world of performance. He opened a shop to build high-powered SK ski boats under the name of "Brendell Boats." But his brother Mike bought a 352-powered Ford in 1960 and the brothers went back to drag racing every weekend. They beefed up the suspension and gearbox linkages and tweaked the motor. It performed consistently and won several events.

Ford's Performance Division man, Fran Hernandez, took note of the Landy boys' winning ways. He offered them limited factory support in the form of special performance items. This supplemented their wins, but in 1961, when Ford introduced the 300-hp, 390-ci, they were out of the running with their 352 V-8.

They made an arrangement with a car dealer, Andy Andrews from Van Nuys: he would provide the car, Dick would provide the performance parts from Ford and the Landys would race it. Andrews was a first-rate wheeler-dealer, Dick recalled, and from his used car lot, you could buy any of the three major manufacturers' high-performance cars brand new.

The yellow 1962 Galaxie 500 two-door sedan from Andy Andrews Ford ran in the Super Stock Class and did well, building a solid reputation for Dick and generating excellent exposure for Andrews.

The team raced so well that Hernandez approached them with a new car that Ford had built as one of the first lightweights of the period. It came with no proof-coating and no accessories, making it the lightest car Ford could build in that body. It was powered by the new 406-ci V-8 and came with tri-power carburetion. It was a dependable and fast car, but when Chevrolet arrived on the scene early that season with a new 409-ci V-8, Dick knew he was dead in the water.

Around this time, he was nicknamed "Dandy Dick" by *Hot Rod* magazine Editor Eric Dalquist,

Here's an at-speed look at the 1964 Automotive Research Dodge super stock factory lightweight Dick raced.

who noted that Dick and his team always dressed in white pants and tennis shoes, which gave them a "Dapper Dan" appearance.

Dick opened his own tuning and engine research shop named "Automotive Research" on Magnolia Avenue in Sherman Oaks. He worked sixteen hours a day, using his new dyno to tune street cars and work on his race cars.

He had done an excellent job with the Fords, and other manufacturers took note. Ronnie Householder from Chrysler's Product Planning Office offered Dick a free new Chrysler to race. At first Dick was apprehensive, but Householder took him on a quick trip to corporate headquarters for a look at the future of Chrysler performance. The trip opened Dick's eyes to the enormous potential of the 413-ci Maxi-Wedge and the Hemi, and from then on Dick and Chrysler were like bread and butter.

In mid-season, he switched from the Ford to a special 1962 413 Maxi-Wedge-powered Dodge Polara 500, a two-door hardtop the company was building for Super Stock racing. It proved to be the best move Dick ever made, and it was the start of a corporate association that grew and lasted for more than twenty years.

The 1962 Dodge was among the first of the Cross-Ram manifold-powered cars. It was extremely fast and produced excellent results on the strip, but it had some teething problems with the T-85 three-speed stick shift. The transmission was not designed for performance applications since the weight of the first gear member made it impossible to shift rapidly. Dick's first outing at Fontana showed that the T-85 was a disastrous choice. He slammed the gearbox through the gears and managed to spit the flywheel

Two pots are better than one. This is a look at the Hemi engine in Dick's 1971 pro stock Dodge Challenger.

out from under the car, cutting a hole through the side panel as it left the driveline.

By the next weekend, he had installed a Torqueflite 727 automatic transmission with special bands, clutches and a shift kit. It proved to be just the tonic

In 1965, Dick hurled his fuel-injected, altered-wheelbase Dodge down the quarter at 165 mph in 9.40 seconds.

the Maxi-Wedge needed. His Mopar showed its muscle, and Dick became difficult to beat as he toured the West Coast, racing at every drag strip that hung out a banner. In 1963, Plymouth gave him a new 426 Maxi-Wedge with an alloy nose, and Dick continued to develop the cars and his talent as one of the fastest men down the Super Stock quarter-mile.

In 1964, Dodge decided that it, too, wanted to get into the performance and drag racing game. With Householder's approval, Dick swapped divisions. It didn't seem to matter to Householder who Dick raced for as long as it was a Chrysler division. Dick worked with Bob Cahill but still maintained access to the development work he had done through Householder and his crew at Chrysler's Product Planning Office.

In early 1964, Dick was still running a one-car team. He used the aluminum-nosed wedge car until Dodge produced a Hemi-powered version halfway through the season, when he became a two-car team. Initially, the Hemi had many teething problems. The first heads were porous and had a thin wall section that collapsed on many occasions. These heads had

never been designed to run at 13:1 compression, and even though they had been fine for NASCAR racing, Dick was punching the tops out of the combustion chambers under the hefty load that his high-compression version cranked out.

It took the factory about six months to redesign the foundry casting so the head had a much thicker section over the combustion chamber, and it eliminated the problem completely. The next problem came from the oiling system, but gradually Dick made the Hemi a very reliable and potent race motor.

In 1964, he came under the sponsorship wing of the L.A. Dodge Dealer's Association with the two new Dodges he ran that year. He earned full factory sponsorship from Chrysler in 1965, and it was with his "Landy's-Dodge" F/X Hemi Super Stock that he became one of hot rodding's most famous drag racers. With that Unlimited F/X Super Stocker, Dick and his crew of three, which included his brother Mike, rolled up nearly 100,000 miles touring the country. Monk Reynolds had set up a midwestern tour, and Dick proceeded to match race his way into

The cigar and the pose. Dick is shown with his 1965 altered-wheelbase Automotive Research Dodge Hemi.

the history books with his Dodges, winning thirty-nine of forty match races and five of seven major competition meets.

Dick ran in the Super Stock class until the end of the 1964 season, but in 1965, with the altered wheelbase cars, he switched to match racing, making a good living by participating in match races from California to Texas. For four months, the team had its headquarters in Arlington, Virginia, racing up to three or four times a week in a five-hundred-mile radius around Arlington. Dick could collect appearance money here because he was the West Coast champion, and he earned cash by winning match races.

The NHRA rules had not kept up with the rapidly changing nature of the Super Stock cars, so Dick ran instead on IHRA tracks. NHRA had outlawed altered-wheelbase AF/X cars. Dick had become a big crowd pleaser, especially when his 1965 altered-wheelbase Dodge consistently turned 9.40–second passes at 165 mph.

During the race recess in the winter of 1966, Dick built a new Logghe chassis race car. Running a supercharged 427, they took the car to the Fresno Drag Strip, where they spent a week testing it. During this intensive testing period, they destroyed three transmissions, and when one transmission exploded, the car caught on fire, severely burning Dick's leg. But they had managed an eight-second pass at 196 mph.

Bob Cahill from Chrysler watched the testing, but when he saw the fire race through the funny car and saw Dick's burns, he made a decision that changed the course of Dick's life. Cahill felt a great accountability toward his team and simply said, "I don't want to be responsible for all this. We're going to do something else."

Dick ran with his radical Dart Funny Cars for a while in 1966. One was an injected Hemi and the other a supercharged Hemi. At the beginning of the season, Dick did well, but then "Dyno" Don Nicholson arrived on the scene with the first tube-framed

Dick and his team were on tour when this shot was taken in 1967. Dick poses up front with the Maxi Wedge while the Hemi sits on the transporter.

Cigar firmly between his teeth, front wheels off the ground, rear tires chewing up the pavement, it's Dick Landy in his Hemi-powered Challenger.

flip-top Funny Car, which proceeded to clean up on the competition. Dick was unhappy about the cars, even though they had logged some sparkling performances early in the season. He felt they were inadequate for the performance potential they had shown.

Early that season, Chrysler had met with Dick and the Sox and Martin team, and came up with a new program. The team decided to let Nicholson have an "open season" at the track with his Funny Car and they would return to Super Stocks.

Chrysler wanted a program to help the dealers sell new automobiles, and Performance Clinics were introduced. The dealer would advertise that Dandy Dick Landy would be at his dealership to display his cars and speak in the evening. The cars would be on display for several days if the race program permitted as much, and Dick would appear at the dealership in the evening, dressed in a sports coat, white shirt and tie, and give a presentation to anywhere from 300 to 1,500 enthusiastic hot rodders. Dick told them about Chrysler high-performance parts, answered questions and showed movies on his drag racing efforts with Chrysler products. The dealers loved it. The program brought buyers into the showroom and was just the kind of response that Chrysler and the dealers wanted. It's important to note that Dick's Performance Clinics were the grassroots of

Chrysler's Direct Connection parts program, which still exists today.

Dick traveled to hundreds of Chrysler dealerships all over the country. His name was a top draw in the showroom, as well as at the track. He presented over 300 clinics during the program's three years.

He had become a man of influence and was invited to private luncheons with the president of Chrysler several times a year. At these meetings, he successfully lobbied for production changes on the street cars, changes the engineers had not been able to get made. Dick was partly responsible for a new four-speed transmission and a new series of lower-ratio gears.

1967 was the year of Dick's return to Super Stocks, with a new R/T 440 Magnum on NHRA tracks. Chrysler provided street Maxi-Wedge and Hemi versions in 1967 and 1968 in a variety of bodies including a Dart, a Charger and Coronet. This got Dick back racing cars and also opened up a new world of paid professional drag racers. Buddy Martin and Dick set up a program using seven major sponsors and, as Dick commented, "It was the first time that Super Stock drag racers ever got paid real money."

Dick was well-equipped with a transporter and crew, and he got new cars every year from Chrysler. 1970 brought a Hemi Challenger, and the NHRA made new rules for Pro-Stock, which made his cars non-competitive in the class. He continued to run through 1974, becoming World Point Champion in AHRA in 1973 and 1974. His racing career ended in 1980, when he finally called it quits after the NHRA made it impossible for the Hemi to continue as a competitive race engine in Pro-Stock.

Since then Dick has developed "Dick Landy Industries" into a research and development company in Northridge, California. There, he makes super-duty valve train gear for top fuel dragsters, does engine development work for a number of major manufacturers and sells a variety of top-quality Hemi parts, including a street piston that is considered the best on the market.

One final point: Dandy Dick Landy always had a ten-inch cigar stuck firmly into the left-hand corner of his mouth. It was there when he raced and there when he worked and talked—but he never smoked it. Dick just calmly rolled it around the corner of his mouth, a sort of security blanket that he has always used for thinking straight and winning races.

Chapter 18

Tom Medley

Tom Medley is a hot rod legend who made his name with his great hands and quick wit instead of with fast cars. While other greats were building the famous cars and running the legendary races, Tom—who came to be known as Stroker McGurk (more on that later)—was enriching the sport helping to publish news of these greats for car buffs across the country and around the world.

Tom was born in 1920, in Lebanon, Oregon, the Strawberry Capital of the World. From the get-go,

An early look at Tom in the famous Stroker McGurk cap.

Here's young Soapbox Tom with his winning entry from the derby in Salem, Oregon.

Tom, in glasses, jokes with the Hot Rod *magazine staff about this modified Mopar special with the inverted 1934 Ford bumper.*

he was an utter car nut, and was particularly fascinated by modified cars.

He amassed a huge collection of newspaper and magazine clippings to chronicle race history when he was a youth, and he spent hours at the Collier Motor Company, where he listened in on drivers talking about racing at Ascot, Gilmore and Gresham speedways.

By the time he was twelve, his hands—or, in particular, his thumbs—helped him feed his hunger for racing. He hitchhiked to and from the races each Thursday night—130 miles each way—just so he could watch the cars at Portland's Gresham Speedway. This meant he didn't get home until nearly 3:00 a.m. on Fridays during race season, but Tom had an incurable bug, "Racing Fever," and watching the fast cars was the only cure.

These were the golden days of "Fronty" Fords and Cragar-headed A engines. Tom was still just a

kid kicking about the pits at the speedways when the first Soapbox Derby was announced; he pounced on the idea and nailed together an entry for the Portland race. He did very well, with his car losing by only one-tenth of a second in the final.

Tom remembered the family cars. First was a Star Touring and later a '29 Chevy two-door sedan, which Tom inherited as his first wheels.

As a teenager, Tom worked twelve-hour shifts in the canneries during the summers, earning enough to buy a few different automobiles. The rest of the time, he played Grade A basketball. His buddy owned a 1934 Ford roadster and Tom badly wanted the car. He was artistic—drawing and illustrating—and he played top-rate basketball. He played so well, in fact, that he won a basketball scholarship to Fullerton Junior College, which paid him $60 a month. With that scholarship, he moved to California, where he attended art classes and played college basketball. The draft had begun for World War II and Tom knew he would be eligible for the armed service. He stayed as long as possible at Fullerton, playing basketball, working on his art and cartooning for the college newspaper. California had opened his eyes and Tom was in love. Having seen the fenderless hot rods race, he became a member of the Night Riders Hot Rod Club and was bitten by the dry lakes racing bug. His life was forever changed.

"Tennis Shoe Tom," the Kart King, takes on another assignment as editor of Hot Rod.

In 1950, Hot Rod *magazine set up this car to run with cars making speed runs to catch the action on film.*

Like all great love affairs, it had its ups and downs. World War II curtailed the crazy side of life as Tom returned to Seattle to work in the Boeing sheet metal shop. He eventually bought a car, but soon replaced it with his first "real" hot rod. Tom found a California-style, fenderless 1929 Ford A V–8 parked on a side street in Portland. He managed to talk the owner out of it for $125. He liked the rasp of the V–8 and, as with his buddy's '34, he had "a taste" for it.

This car didn't last long. Tom managed to center-punch a power pole with the roadster one night and it ended up at Al Cooper's Speedshop. Tom took a second job at Cooper's to try to bail the roadster out (something he never managed to do).

He was drafted into the Army and did his basic training at Cheyenne, Wyoming. His aptitude test confused the Army enlistment personnel, as it showed 50% mechanical and 50% art skills. They had to compromise, and Tom ended up in motor mechanics' school for three months.

From there, he was assigned to the 778th Ordinance Division in Durham, North Carolina. He was moved to the 311th Infantry Division as the riding mechanic on a Howitzer cannon pulled behind a Jeep.

It didn't take long before Tom's artistic training drew attention. The mail he sent home was decorated with drawings and cartoons, and it caught the eye of an officer at headquarters. Tom was transferred to the headquarters training section, where he did his first cartoon series, "Fearless Freddie Flash," Stroker McGurk's predecessor.

By no means did this slight diversion mean that Tom would sit out the war drawing cartoons. He was soon mobilized and sent to Tennessee for winter maneuvers. On Thanksgiving 1944, he shipped out to England for LST training; from there, he went to France, served in the Battle of the Bulge and was among the first over the Rhine. Tom continued to play basketball at every opportunity. At one point, he played three miles from the front line in an old school gym in Germany.

When the war ended, Tom ran a small photo lab at the airforce base in Berlin. They also dabbled in the black market to make a few bucks to spend back home, and played basketball in old blimp hangars.

Tom had not forgotten hot rods. During his time in Europe, Veda Orr from Culver City had kept him and the rest of the Southern California Timing Association members in the military up to date with the *SCTA News*. This was a vital link, and many men in

Here's an example of a "Stroker McGurk" cartoon from 1953. Tom's humor struck a chord with every hot rodder.

They could identify with the situations and foul-ups his cartoons portrayed.

107

the military felt a great admiration for Veda's dedication. When Tom came home, he tried to interest Veda in starting a hot rod magazine, but she declined, and Tom went back to college at the L.A. Art Center to finish his advertising design coursework.

Tom married and moved back to Portland, where he worked as an apprentice for an automotive upholsterer. He learned to tuck and roll, build a Carson top and stitch up an interior. Southern California was still a magnet for Tom, though, and within eighteen months, he had returned to resume his studies at the Art Center. Tom hung out with the hot rod crowd and dabbled in cartoons. He had popped a few cartoons on the Blair's Speed Shop notice board in Pasadena, where one of his Oregon buddies, "Tim" Timmerman, worked. Pete Petersen saw Tom's cartoon work and they started talking. Tom became a Petersen Publishing staffer, doing layouts, writing the humor section and helping Al Isaacs sell ads. Petersen also discovered that Tom was a top-flight photographer. Tom had brought back from Germany a Super Conta-A 120 roll film camera, which was superb for automotive work. Bob D' Olivo came to work for Petersen and the two men

Tom Medley, 1990.

covered Bonneville, the speedways, the Mexican Road Race, the technical stories and economy runs.

On his first trip to Bonneville, Tom brought along a portable darkroom and processed his film in the desert, just to be sure he was returning with the right results. His work graced the pages of *Hot Rod* magazine and helped to develop a style that today helps it remain one of the world's leading automotive publications. His images were well-composed and, where possible, told a story instead of just presenting a scene. For several years, Petersen also commissioned him to make a 16 mm movie of Bonneville.

His work at Petersen flourished in other directions, too. His cartoon character, "Stroker McGurk" "sort of evolved," according to Tom. His natural affinity for drawing led him to start cartooning hot rodding and hot rodders. Stroker McGurk quickly became hot rodding's best-known home mechanic and alter ego, and Tom became known as "Stroker."

Trips to Bonneville became regular events. Tom's favorite story concerning Bonneville is about getting there. Traveling back from Bonneville with Racer Brown and Wally Parks in the early-fifties, Tom and Parks spent many hours shooting jack rabbits and heading down side roads looking for vintage tin, much to Brown's dismay because Racer just wanted to go home. Between them, all they had was a credit card good for gas only, sixty-eight cents in change, a loaf of bread, a bottle of mayonnaise and a package of baloney. They made it home, happy, hungry and broke.

Tom's work with Petersen diversified and flowered as the Petersen empire grew. He was offered the editorship of *Hot Rod* magazine several times, but declined it for personal reasons. Into the late-sixties, he became publisher of *Rod and Custom* magazine at Petersen. Eventually, *Rod and Custom* was absorbed into *Hot Rod* magazine, leaving a gap in the magazine industry for a pure hot rod magazine. This gap was filled by yet another man of talent, Tom McMullen, with his *Street Rodder* magazine.

While in charge at *Rod and Custom*, Tom coined the phrase, "Street is Neat," which became the motto of the National Street Rod Association. He traveled extensively to represent the magazine, and was a guest at many hot rod events. He still had time for fooling with his hot rods, building engines and hitting the road to attend yet another event.

In fact, one of his other favorite stories is about getting to an event. Ron Waite, Dennis Varney and Tom were headed out to an event late one Saturday when the water pump in Waite's F–100 quit after climbing a long grade. They pulled into a small desert town, blowing steam, and it looked as though they'd never get to the event in time. Ten minutes later while they were still looking under the hood, a kid of about twelve appeared and asked what had happened to the truck. Fifteen minutes later the kid reappeared with a still-warm F–100 water pump in his hand. The guys looked at each other and no one asked any questions. They bolted the water pump into the truck, gave the kid $5 and continued on their way, figuring the great Big-Block God was looking after them.

Tom continued to cartoon, write and photograph for *Hot Rod* through the seventies and into the early-eighties. His talents were then directed into other areas of the corporation, managing the library and video department. In 1985, Chevrolet selected him for its "Legends of Performance" magazine award for contributions to hot rodding.

After thirty-seven years of working for Petersen, Tom retired in 1986 to stay home and finish his maroon 1940 Ford coupe powered with a 350 Chevy small-block V–8. He has been called the "hot rodder's hot rodder," and is widely loved and revered as one of hot rodding's neatest people.

Some sixties cruising in a good-looking hiboy.

Chapter 19

Bruce Meyers

Bruce shown testing the first Towd at Baja.

The Bruce Meyers story is one which no children's toy manufacturer wants told. That's because Meyers received no toys when he was a child, and instead, his parents gave him tools and told him to build things for himself. This opened the door of his creativity and helped him teach himself the basics of many creative skills that let him become a major success in the hot rod and dune buggy business.

If more parents realized how Bruce's life was enriched by his having to make his own playthings, they would buy their children tools, not tops, dolls and balls.

Meyers was blessed with talented parents. His father was the first man to sell dealership franchises for Henry Ford, and his mother was renowned singer Peggy O'Neill. They encouraged his creativity, and he developed it, giving him the skills to spearhead projects ranging from making dune buggies to building a fantastic house in Mexico.

Today he looks tan, fit and rugged with his short crop of hair and tan skin. He looks like an ex-football player in his late forties, yet he's in his sixties. He has been through great highs and spirit-challenging lows during his career, a career whose automotive ties go back to his years as a West Coast teen.

Bruce was a typical southern California teenager: hanging out, cruising and drag racing 1934 Fords on the dry lakes on the weekends. After a stint in the Navy during World War II, which included surviving a kamikazi attack on the aircraft carrier Bunker Hill and a severe bout of rheumatic fever, Bruce was ready to go back to the Californian lifestyle by the sea. He loved sailing and when he was offered a trip to the South Seas, jumped at the chance to sail to Tahiti and build a trading post in the Cook Islands.

Once back in California, he designed his own boat, a forty-two-foot catamaran. The project took several years to complete, but when finished, it turned out to be one of the fastest multi-hulls around, winning the Newport to Ensenada race in its first try from the back of the field. While building his catamaran, Bruce earned a living by working on other fiberglass boat projects, especially the California Series of Yachts by Bill Lapworth.

For the Lapworth boats, Meyers built the tooling and molds. They were huge molds of up to forty feet long, twenty feet high, and twenty-eight feet wide. Bruce's work with these boats led to other fiberglass products and he became an expert on molding fiberglass on a large scale. He developed roll-over molds and several other critical techniques for building large boats, techniques now used industry-wide.

Being close to the sea, Bruce was a surfer, shaping boards as a side-line and hitting the curls when the surf was up. Bruce also loved VW Kombi buses and, with his wife Shirley, would explore Baja and the West Coast, surfing, diving and fishing. One day they went roaming along Pismo Beach in a sand sailer and Bruce noticed that off in the dunes were other vehicles called "Dune Buggies."

These buggies were stripped down and shortened chassis powered by V–8 engines (some were

The first street-worthy Towd.

VW-powered), but were nothing fancy. They were all home-built and crude, but they got Bruce thinking that they could be modified in a much simpler way, and it would be fun to work on them.

Bruce modified his VW Kombi bus with cut-out wheel wells and bigger tires. The wheels he popped out at home were made by fitting the VW centers to

Bruce pounds one of the first Manx vehicles over the dunes at Pismo Beach, California.

111

The first Meyers Manx takes shape in Bruce's Costa Mesa shop.

scrapyard Buick rims fitted with 9.50 × 15 tires. (That may not sound like such a big deal today, but in 1962, it was a revolution!) His bus was known affectionately as the "Little Red Riding Bus." Suddenly, it went from being their only transportation to being a dune jumper. It became the catalyst that let Bruce and Shirley travel far and wide into territory they'd not been able to reach before. But it had its limitations. Bruce decided that there was something to this

Bruce Meyers (left) and Ted Mangels (right) are shown during their trip to plan the first Baja 1,000 Mexican road race.

lightweight, rear-engined, big-tire idea, and set out to build a vehicle that would be suited to doing what he wanted to do: have fun on the beach and in the back country.

Several months of sketching, brainstorming and fiddling produced a design that he could build with simple tools. Bruce built a small-scale model in clay. His design was the outcome of his thoughts, the VW Schwimmwagen and the cartoon cars from several comic strips.

The design used a fiberglass body with an integral steel frame glassed into the body. Attached to the frame were the VW suspension, steering and powertrain. In August 1963, Bruce started work on a heap of clay over a wooden frame, building a buck to make a mold. Little did he realize at the time that he would start a worldwide trend with his little fun car. In fact, he started a whole new industry—fiberglass dune buggies.

The first body was pulled from the mold in May 1964. There were twelve cars in the first batch and they had one problem: the price of $985 was a big whack for just the kit, yet Bruce was losing money at that price. He had to think the project out some more. Interest in the car was fantastic, and Bruce quickly realized that the solution to his dilemma was to use a shortened VW platform.

This idea was the breakthrough. Others had used the VW running gear before—Bill Devin had designed and built the Devin D in 1957 using VW components—but what Bruce accomplished in that one brilliant flash was to start the off-road revolution spinning at 100 mph. It made it possible to have an effective off-road vehicle for a few hundred dollars and put it together yourself.

Steve McQueen drove this customized Corvair-powered Manx in the film, "The Thomas Crown Affair."

Bruce's good work came together in the Manx. Anyone could buy one, anyone could build one and everyone wanted one. What a marketing opportunity! Not even Madison Avenue advertising agencies could have stirred up as much interest in a vehicle as the Manx did for itself.

There were plenty of cheap VWs available. Bruce and his investors, Elaine and John Bond of *Road & Track* fame, were onto a hot new product, which they named the "Meyers Manx." You could have it in any form, from basic kit to a finished car from the factory.

The Manx was an ideal use of the aging VW and its use in the buggy enhanced every aspect of the VW. In one swift shift, it made the Beetle into a butterfly. The car performed better, handled better, had a smaller turning radius and was extremely nimble to drive. It also put to good use the trailing arm rear suspension that had been designed for the North African desert during World War II.

On the street, the Manx's light weight and easy handling quickly made it the favorite set of wheels to be seen in, from Costa Mesa to Newfoundland. The buff magazines found a new hero in the Manx, and around Bruce's studio today are numerous covers and features on the vehicle. It was featured on the covers of *Hot Rod, Car and Driver* and many other publications. News of the Manx spread like wildfire, and hundreds of pages were dedicated to the Manx in magazines all over the world. Its cuteness caught the marketplace at the right time, and if "hip" is the correct term for 1964, the Manx was so hip that it "out-hipped" the rest.

The Manx flowered overnight and with it came money, fame and fun. Baja had long held a great attraction for Bruce. With his good friend Ted Mangels, he surveyed a race to the tip of Baja. During the return trip, the pair managed a new record: thirty-four hours and forty-five minutes from La Paz to Tijuana. It was actually an hour shorter, but to get an official to record the time, they had to wait for the Tourist Office to open.

Within a short time, two off-road organizations—NORRA and SCORE—were formed. Ed Pearlman appointed himself chairman of NORRA and Bruce became one of the charter members.

The Manx spawned a whole new aftermarket: wheels, tires, roll bars, metallic finishes and other VW performance parts. If you are old enough to remember when the "Mod Squad" ruled, you might remember the flowered vinyl tops that General Motors offered as an option in 1968. Bruce had his "Mod Manx" on display at the Pan-Pacific Auditorium in April 1967, where a group of GM executives spent considerable time examining the car. (It was stuck in the lobby because the service elevator was too small to carry it to its assigned exhibit space.)

Not only was it a car for the guy in the street and at the beach, it was a car coveted by the stars. Steve

The Manx SR–2, the second-generation Manx, was more like a sports car than a dune buggy.

McQueen had one with a hot Corvair engine and custom bodywork in the "Thomas Crown Affair." Elvis used one in several movies, and Paul Newman drove one. Another high point in this illustrious little car's life was its acceptance as an art piece by the L.A. County Art Museum in the California Design Competition. And Bruce was asked to provide a car for the 1968 World's Fair in Tokyo.

The military also wanted a look at this unusual vehicle. The armies of Peru and Israel bought their share for evaluation. Other products followed: the Towd, an off-road racing buggy; the Towdster, a family buggy; and the gorgeous SR sports.

By 1971, the B. F. Meyers Company employed seventy to eighty people, but Bruce and Shirley felt the terrible strains of running the business. They had built over 7,000 Manxes, 250 Towds and 250 SRs, and their sales network had more than 200 dealers across

Bruce with his scrapbook in his office.

Bruce Meyers

adventures. For one thing, he needed space to demonstrate his buggies to distributors and customers. He negotiated with the Irvine Company and leased Saddleback as the first off-road and motorcycle park.

The fiberglass industry has endured some fairly frightening horror stories over the years, and for Bruce, the worst was when the competition was able to copy his ideas and designs at will. Bruce went to court over the massive patent infringement by several hundred overnight buggy manufacturers. He lost a landmark patent infringement case because of an unsympathetic judge. Bruce felt the judge was more worried about the clock on the wall than the case he had before him.

Dejected and annoyed, Bruce wanted to call it a day. The day-to-day operations of the company had grown at an incredible pace and were becoming unmanageable. Bruce felt they were always off balance and never really able to catch up before the next test presented itself. The IRS closed in and took a huge share of company funds, forcing Bruce and Shirley to sell their home. The company was liquidated and sold. The day of the sale, Bruce recalled, was a very unhappy time. "The yard was a sea of high-dollar molds, all of which were sold for $250." Bruce and Shirley separated and started their lives afresh.

The Meyers Manx project had come to an end (maybe not the end it deserved), but it still is considered the best kit car ever made. Bruce recalled that one of the most heartwarming tales to come out of those years was when Pete Brock of Carroll Shelby Racing fame said to him, "You know, Bruce, I've had my cars on magazine covers all over the world, but what you have done is something only a handful of car builders have ever done. You put one of your cars on every street."

Today, Bruce lives with his wife Winnie in Valley Center, California, not far from where he was so deeply involved in the Manx project. He's working on a revolutionary series of ocean sculptures, which will be done the Meyers way.

the nation. In five years, they had gone from a one-man, one-stall garage to a high-dollar company.

During this time, Bruce spent many hours racing and proving his product in Baja. During one race, he badly crashed his Towd into a solid earth bank, breaking both his legs. It took twenty hours to get him back to California for medical treatment, and twenty years later, he still walks with a slight limp. When he recovered, he decided it was time for new

Chapter 20

Ak Miller

Akton "Ak" Miller never met a terrain on which he didn't like to race. Whether it was the dry lakes, the Bonneville Salt Flats, the incredibly challenging and unforgiving deserts of Mexico or the thin-air climb up Pikes Peak, Ak loved them all because he simply loved to race.

The highly admirable thing about Ak is that he wasn't a self-centered, me-first racer. He wasn't only concerned with his cars or his getting to drive. He was concerned with the good of the sport, and worked tirelessly without pay for years to get hot rodders and drag racers organized and united. He realized that without a solid image and a united front, the sport's racers might lose their access to popular driving spots. He was one of the leaders who worked to head that off by seeking out sites that were good for racing and where the participants, their friends and fans would be welcome.

One of the early 260-ci Cobra racers found its way to Bonneville and Ak drove it to a Class C record. It had an exotic air scoop out front while Ak wore an exotic sun-blocking hat up top.

Ak at the wheel of a streamlined 1927 T Bonneville road-ster in 1952. The car used a V–8 90 and Moon discs. Dean Moon

If the varieties of terrain on which Ak raced sound varied, consider the difference in landscapes between his native Denmark and Pico Rivera, a town in the midst of California's old oil fields. The Miller family emigrated from Denmark to California in 1925, hoping for a share in the perceived riches of the new land. Ak, only five years old at the time of the move, attended school with his three brothers and two sisters while his father toiled in the oil fields until the Depression hit.

The Depression hit California's oil fields like a sledge hammer on an empty bean can. Ak's father

This is a 1953 modified, dual-point distributor Ak crafted. Dean Moon

116

lost his job, and the children left school to try to earn all they could to help the family get by, except Ak, who was too young and who stayed in class.

When Ak was a teenager, he got a job in Whittier, California, at the Nixon Grocery Store. He worked for Hanna Nixon, mother of eventual-President Richard Nixon.

During these early teenage years Ak developed his taste for mechanics. With his three brothers, he "messed around with Model Ts and Chevys." They became part of the first hot rod crowd. Ak tried his hand at building a car. His first cars were Chevy roadsters running stock fours and sixes; then he added a little heat with some high-performance items: Winfield cam, carburetors and a shaved head.

It wasn't long before the brothers got a lot more serious. In 1935 they belonged to the Road Runner's Car Club. They built a 1928 Chevy roadster for the dry lakes that featured a modified Chevy four with a Winfield cam and Tornado head. The timing at the lakes was done with compression hose timing traps owned by George Wight, the proprietor of Bell Auto Parts.

At their first dry lakes run, one of Ak's brothers was all set to drive the Chevy, but in a moment of trepidation, he handed the wheel over to Ak, who, at

fifteen and unlicensed, was the illogical choice in many ways, but he had a leather helmet, goggles, a scarf and no fear. "I felt like the Red Baron going into battle," he said. He had never driven on the lakes before, and ran the Chevy down the mile course, going through the traps at 94 mph. They positioned six race cars to run abreast over the course. Ak had the pole and used it to his advantage until about three-quarters of a mile down the course, the condenser fell off and he was passed by the other five cars—leaving him to "eat their dust."

Ak had caught the speed bug. He wanted to go fast, really fast. During this time, they were kicked off Muroc and the clubs moved to Harper and Lucerne dry lakes. The roots of the early hot rod clubs were planted. During the weekend, they would partake in friendly rivalry on the streets. Ak raced his 1931 Chevy roadster in Pasadena, on Westminster Fifth Avenue, Telegraph and Broadway.

Ak's Chevy wasn't a box stocker; it was a proper hot rod. At first, he ran a 320–ci Buick straight–8 overhead valve. He replaced that with a Cadillac 346 V–8. He shaved the heads, installed a Winfield cam and built a modified Pierce-Arrow dual-point distributor. He modified it as a double four-cylinder

During a break in the Carrera Pan-Americana race in 1953, Ak (at rear of car) spends some time with youngsters eager *to get a look at the car, the Cabello de Hierro, the "Horse of Iron."*

distributor which, in turn, gave him plenty of dwell time and worked beautifully on the slow revving 150–hp Cadillac. The Chevy turned 118 mph on the dry lakes and 105 mph for the quarter.

Other cars rapidly followed. He modified a 1932 Ford roadster with a similar Cadillac L-head engine. Running on used Indy tires at the lakes, Ak managed to turn up the wick and put the "Fordillac" through the traps at 128 mph. Not a bad effort for a nineteen-year-old.

When World War II reared its ugly head, the lakes closed down. Being a native son of Denmark, Ak was initially rejected from military service but the situation quickly changed. He was naturalized and inducted into the military, trained and sent to Europe. He served in the Second Armored Division, fighting in the infamous Battle of the Bulge.

The rigors of war took their toll on Ak and after the Battle of the Bulge he was taken to a British hospital for six months. Upon his release from the hospital, he was transported back to the United States and discharged in Colorado Springs. What better place for a guy with hot rods in his blood to spend a little time? Pikes Peak was just half an hour out of town. One good look at the Peak and a couple of turns up the hill convinced Ak that he would return and race Pikes Peak.

When many of the old lakes racers returned after the war, Wally Parks reformed the Road Runners. Soon, other hot rod clubs formed again. Ak recalled that there were thirty to forty clubs in the L.A. area in the late-forties. Ak became president of the Southern California Timing Association (SCTA) and served in that capacity for three years.

With Parks, Pete Petersen and Bob Barsky, he organized the first hot rod show in the Exposition Armory in Los Angeles. The show was financially rewarding for the SCTA treasury, but it created a problem: it was so successful that one entrepreneur wanted to own the "Hot Rod" name and show scene. But Ak and the SCTA would have none of it, and the outcome was significant. The SCTA gave the name Hot Rod to Pete Petersen for his "little rag" newsletter because, as Ak figured, Petersen was there to help the sport. It was a decision that showed Ak's perceptive vision of the future.

The SCTA had money in the bank, which was a new feeling, but the group was "running out of real estate, or a place to race," recalled Ak. By 1947, the dry lakes crowd was large, and forty to fifty people worked on the safety patrol. Ak, Pete Petersen and Parks sought a new location for the lakes meet. They covered every possible lake between Palmdale and Las Vegas and found nothing. Parks decided that the Bonneville Salt Lake in the Great Salt Lake Desert on the Utah-Nevada border would be just the right place for speed trials. Despite some opposition from club members who thought that Bonneville was too

Three great racers are shown with their wives. The racers are (l-r) Ak (with his wife Della), Bobby Unser and Parnelli Jones. The event is the 1963 Pikes Peak hillclimb.

far away, Parks and Ak went to Salt Lake City, where they negotiated the use of the flats for a one-week speed trial. The Salt has been the major yearly event for the SCTA ever since.

Sixty entrants turned up for the first Bonneville Speed Week. Ak remembered all the hard planning and work that went into making the event happen, how he met opposition and how they lost their shirts on the first event to the tune of $168. But it proved to the members that Bonneville was the only place to hold Speed Week. The club made its money back the next year and Bonneville grew in stature and profitability.

Ak was not one to sit back and just run an event; he had to be part of it, too. In the first year of the event, he raced a 1927 T roadster that used a mid-mounted Ford flathead and had a custom-built chassis using four-wheel, independent suspension riding on torsion bars. Ak fabricated the entire chassis, including building his own U-joints. The roadster ran 178 mph. In 1952, he came back as one of the 125 entrants but with another idea: three racers in one. He ran in three classes, using three different engines. He needed thirty minutes to change engines. He won three class records, with speeds of 136 mph, a 158 mph and a 178 mph.

These were the days of shoestring racing—no motorhomes or fancy accommodations, but guys with just enough money to get to Bonneville, buy their tow car gas from Earl's Texaco, race a few times, sleep in the old Air Force bunkhouse at the airport and wash in the water supply tank for Wendover.

In 1953, Ak returned with a Wally Parks T roadster. The flathead was stock, except for the carburetor and cam. With Charlie Day as mechanic, Ak hot-shoed the roadster down the Salt four times, producing exactly the same time of 123.456 mph on each run. After some discussion with the official timer, Ak figured they were either misreading the clocks or there was some other technical error. But on his fifth run, the round-nosed racer produced 128 mph and his speed jinx was broken.

Ak was fascinated by anything that went fast. Sports cars soon came into play and he was asked to prepare a car for the up-and-coming Carrera Pan-American Road Race, designed to celebrate the opening of the Pan-American Highway. A so-called famous Mexican race car driver had been contracted to drive the car.

When the time came for the test session, Ak took the driver for a little run down the street. Ak crested the first hump in the road at around 100 mph, lifting the car clear off the ground. To say Ak scared the living daylights out of his passenger would be putting it mildly! The Mexican race car drive swore that he would never ride again with the "crazy Americano." The real meat of this story was that Ak was again in the right place at the right time. With Doug

In 1970, Ak piloted this Devin to a class victory in the Pikes Peak hillclimb as daring observers and photographers captured the dusty action on film from the edge of the road.

Harrison of *Hot Rod* magazine, he drove the race. Unfortunately, they did not finish because the transmission broke and put them out of the race.

In 1953, Ak decided to build his own car. He got the chassis from a friend and fitted a 1949 Ford front end with dual shocks and a transverse-sprung rear end on a Columbia two-speed axle. He modified the chassis to take the Oldsmobile V-8, Cadillac transmission and early Ford rear end. Parks named it "Cabello de Hierro," or "Horse of Iron." It was built on a shoestring, $1,500 budget. The T body was bedecked with the sponsor's artwork, and the famous nose made of chromed electrical conduit gave it a toothy grille.

The Cabello ran great, except for the Ford rear end. After every section of 200 to 300 miles, they had to remove the third member and put in a new gear set, which they bought from the local Ford dealership. This took forty-five minutes and by the time they had finished the race, they were experts in Ford rear ends. On the flat, the Cabello would pull 125 mph, which gave it the ability to run with the Ferrari that Luigi Chinetti had entered. On one 600-mile section, Ak drove by himself since his partner Doug Harrison chose to stay in Leon. On this section, he averaged 90 mph. On one section of fifty arrow-straight miles, Jack McGrath and Clay Smith in the

Ak (No. 311) leads the pack at Monterey, driving his modified Chevy-powered Devin against a Maserati Birdcage.

team Lincoln were drafting him at around the 100–mph mark and waving him on to go faster, but he kept his head and he moved over to let them pass, fearing an early gear failure if he didn't let up.

In Durango, Ray Brock changed the gears and, with Harrison on board, they pressed on. The race had taken them through deserts, jungles and 10,000 feet up into the mountains, where the carburetor iced up so badly that they had to pick the ice off with a screwdriver before continuing. The hot rod Oldsmobile still managed to take eighth place in the 2,000–mile race.

They returned in 1954, with better rubber to race on and a new Spicer rear end that did not need constant work. Bill Stroppe was running the Lincoln team and gave Ak his old tires which still had plenty of life left. They had a new 1935 Nash transmission with a five-pinion overdrive, which proved to be perfect for the job. Before the race, the guys had met a pair of women who had their own car. This proved to be a boon for them, as they could get around without having to drive the race car before the start. On race day, they were invited to be guests of the women's grandparents, who owned a house right at the start line. The grandparents fed and entertained the guys and even called in a priest to bless them. They affixed the patron saint of Mexico to the dash because they claimed he was good for much better mileage than Saint Peter.

They had modified the Cabello with a trick Oldsmobile 260–ci engine that ran low-compression (7.5:1) pistons to cope with the low-octane Mexican gasoline. The sand-cast pistons by Jahns were hard-anodized, so Ak could run the Olds without air cleaners. The engine ran great, consistently cruising on many of the wide-open sections at well over 100 mph. As added insurance against a rear end failure,

Ak came up with a special lubricant consisting of white lead, bean oil and SAE 90 hypoid gear oil. A Mobil lubricant engineer recommended this mixture to Smith.

One of Ak's tales of the race is about Bobby Unser, who was driving a Jaguar. One of the small towns had agreed to have a man wave a lamp to show a ninety-degree turn in the road. Unfortunately, the open exhaust of Unser's Jaguar made so much noise that it frightened the lamp waver and he fled, leaving the corner unmarked. Unser and his navigator didn't make the turn but did manage to make it to the ninth row in the church after clearing the church steps and front door.

The section leading into Mexico City was as spooky as it was fun. The cheering crowd parted like a wave as the Cabello came tearing down the main drag into the city. Spectators were sticking out their feet to see whether they could be run over or were trying to slap the car as it passed at 100 mph. Ak placed fifth against intense competition from Ferraris, Porsches, a Pegaso and a little Italian Ossca.

Ak's Mexican adventures naturally led him into sports car racing, where he achieved an equally impressive record. Jerry Unser became his mentor as Ak prepared a Chevy-powered Devin. Within a short time Ak had the ill-handling Devin tamed. He ran a Chevy engine at first, then an Olds engine and eventually, a Ford engine. The Devin was a primitive beast. It used a transverse rear leaf spring on a Ford rear end and a 1950 Chevy front suspension. Eventually, it would have a fully independent suspension.

In 1957, Ak's love of sports cars got him involved in a project to build a Hemi-powered sports car to contest the Mille Miglia in Italy. This car used a Kurtis Kraft Chassis, 392 Hemi V–8, Jaguar transmission and full torsion-bar suspension. As the car neared completion, it was badly burned in a garage fire, but not enough to stop Ak. He returned to the workshop with his body builder, Briton Jack Sutton, and rebuilt the handmade body. This was the "Cabello II." With no time to test the racer, it was shipped to Italy, where it split one of its high-tech alloy brake drums, putting it out of the race at a very early stage.

"Pikes Peak was skid city, where you held your breath for thirteen minutes," Ak recalled. There's no doubt that Ak had the golden touch for both engines and driving; he won his class ten times in the "Race to the Clouds." He also won the Great Salt Lake Road Race twice with his 427–powered Devin. The race was held at an old airport just outside Salt Lake City. Always one to try something new Ak went back to the Peak in 1971 with a college project they dubbed the "Pikes Peak Mustang." Instead of taking a regular crew along, he took five college kids who helped build the car. They installed one of Ak's 351 Ford Winsor engines, and Ak won the stock car class.

The Mustang was taken to Bonneville in 1971, with the same kids crewing again. Running in classes B and C and using Ford stock components, Ak again cleaned up, setting two course records—much to the objections of his competition. The Mustang ran 175 mph with Ak's 302 V–8 engine and 180 mph on the 351 V–8 that Carroll Shelby Racing loaned him for Speed Week.

Duke Hallock, head of the development lab at AiResearch, was a close friend. He told Ak that turbos were the way to the future for performance cars. In 1972, Hallock sent a couple of small turbos over to Ak for evaluation. With Hallock's help, Ak worked up a system and installed the turbo on a propane-powered Pinto. The results were spectacular for the time; the quick little car turned 105 mph for the quarter-mile and had a hard-to-top speed of 128 mph.

Ak was also working under contract to the Ford Motor Company. Jack Passimo recommended Ak as the man Ford should have on board to help with the youth market. It was initially a one-year contract but became a ten-year project. Ak ran Ford's Custom Car Caravan; wrote Autolite's Muscle Car books; helped in the product planning stages of new models; helped run the Lincoln-Mercury streamliner at Bonneville to a new world class record of 278 mph on a 1,500–cc four-cylinder engine; worked on the press introduction of every new Ford during those years;

and flew hundred of thousands of miles to work the auto shows on Ford's behalf.

Ak loved racing and when he got the chance to go off-road, he went to Baja in a Ford-sponsored Ranchero for the inaugural Baja 1,000. He returned the next year in a custom-built racer F–250 pickup, winning Class 7 hands down. With Brock as co-driver, they managed many major off-road wins in Ford products until Stroppe took over Ford's off-road racing program.

With the demise of the muscle car era and implementation of new EPA air regulations, Ford tightened its belt and Ak returned happily to his private interests in California. He worked on his long-term goals of turbocharging and propane installations for passenger cars. He tested and destroyed many engines during these research projects. Ford asked him to design a propane conversion, which they would eventually sell in Canada. Ak built a turbocharged Fairmont for Donald Petersen, which also turned out to be a winner in one of Ford's research projects.

Today, he runs "Ak Miller Turbocharging" in Pico Rivera. At around seventy years of age, he is still working on his propane/turbo conversions. His personal car is a plain-looking 1985 Thunderbird with propane-feeding twin turbos on a 351 Ford V–8. It may not look like a hot car, but it's what's under the hood that counts—and Ak Miller has always been a man full of surprises when it comes to very fast cars.

Ak won two classes at Bonneville the year he raced this Mustang Bonneville racer. He helped build it, as did a group of college students who called themselves "Collegiate Racing Associates."

Chapter 21

Dean Moon

In the sixties, there was perhaps no sticker more popular than one that said "Moon-Equipped" and had Dean Moon's famous Moon-eyes logo. Hot rodders across the country placed them in prominent spaces on their cars. Teenagers got in trouble for sticking them on their father's cars to look cool on a Friday night's cruise. Boys who built model cars pestered auto shop clerks until they coughed up some Moon stickers for the boys' bikes, notebooks and school lockers.

The popularity didn't stem from Dean Moon having been a marketing genius. It stemmed from the fact that the logo was cool, and the fact that he had earned the respect of drivers he ran with and customers who bought his top-notch performance parts. Since bootleg sticker makers were reproduc-

Dean (right) poses with crew mates and the trophy-winning 1934 "Fordor" sedan at Bonneville in 1952.

ing his logo and stickers from coast-to-coast, Moon didn't get rich from the popularity of his logo and image. Yet he did receive some well-deserved fame and recognition, which is appropriate since he was a determined, hard-working, sometimes hot-headed and sometimes hard-headed individual. He was perhaps the archetypical hot rodder, an independent man who went his own way—usually at top speed behind the wheel of a gorgeous, fire-breathing rod.

Despite his independence and his image as a rebel, Moon was perceptive about the values of getting organized. He didn't believe in forming or joining a group just for the sake of it, but he believed in doing so when it was done for a good reason. That's why he helped forge several vital enthusiast, racer and industry groups during his rich career.

Dean was born in Minnesota, where his father ran a Phillips gas station during Prohibition. To supplement the family income, he also ran moonshine out of the gas station in cans that looked just like gas cans. It was easy: just drop by Pop Moon's Phillips station and get a can of 100 octane.

When he was seven, Dean worked as the delivery boy delivering to the mayor, the police chief, the doctor and much of the community. Dean remembered how the tips got bigger as the weather got colder, and at forty-eight degrees below, business boomed. His father was arrested and fined $75, and the Moon family sold the gas station and moved to California.

It was in the open and rapidly expanding California of the 1930s that the Moon family flourished. Dean's father bought Tessie's Cafe in Santa Fe Springs, which today is revered as one of the birthplaces of hot rodding. Dean worked after school, at night and on weekends as a bus boy and later as a short-order cook in the re-named Moon's Cafe. Santa Fe Springs was where the oil boom movies were filmed: "Black Gold," "Boom Town" and "Gold Town." Dean rubbed shoulders with the greats, busing tables for Clark Gable, Spencer Tracy, Jimmy Cagney and Lana Turner.

Dean (right) hangs out with his pals at the Clock Drive-In. He and his buddies are wearing Strokers Club jackets.

Automobiles were his obsession and by sixteen, Dean was totally infatuated with V–8 roadsters. He loved anything that had the smell of going fast. His sense of automobiles and business led him to making

Shirley Moon sat in Dean's 1926 T Roadster in Pico Rivera.

Dean posed next to an Air Force jet in his days as a U.S.A.F. photographer. His time in the service let him polish his far-reaching skills as a photographer.

123

The first Cobra was built in Moon's workshop. Carroll Shelby is shown at the wheel talking with his secretary, who poses with a tiara on her head for this publicity shot taken at a southern California golf course. The shot was taken shortly after the car was hand-rubbed with Brillo pads to give the sheet metal a shine for photography.

fuel blocks that could deliver equal fuel pressure to multi-carburetor set-ups on flatheads. He fabricated fuel blocks in an old shed behind the Moon Cafe at night and bused tables before school—all while attending Whittier High School with another yet-to-be-famous hot rod rebel, Richard M. Nixon.

Around this period, other pioneers tinkered in sheds and garages all over California. Vic Edelbrock, Sr., was building intake manifolds in an old

The famous Moon Eyes logo, one of the most popular and well-known logos in all of motorsports.

gas station in Beverly Hills; Joe Bailon was customizing cars in San Francisco; and Fred Offenhauser was gaining fame as the man who built bullet-proof engines.

Drive-ins, street racing and cruising were just beginning, and hanging out with hot rods was "it." Dean's cars were fast and he developed a reputation for knowing the right tricks. He sold fuel blocks and some hop-up parts while hanging out at the Hula Hut in Whittier.

During this time, Dean made many street racing forays. Guys cruised in Deuce coupes and roadsters to have a run. It was like a Wild West story of challenging a gun fighter to a duel, but when the dust settled on Telegraph Avenue, there were no bodies with bullet holes—just engines cooling as the racers stopped to relive a race or collect a bet.

Dean used to talk about drag racing down Washington Boulevard which, in the forties, ran through orange groves. One midnight, he was arrested. Fifty supporters joined him in court the next morning, and Judge Merton T. Ray gave him seven days in jail but no fine for drag racing on public streets. He was out four days later and back street racing, only now a bit wiser. Dean was the first hot rodder jailed for drag racing in California.

World War II interrupted Dean's racing activities for a few years. He served in the Merchant Navy throughout the Pacific and in Japan; he was among the first Allied personnel to go into Japan at the end of the war. Dean and his buddies got into all sorts of mischief with the local beer and girls. Dean got a glint in his eyes when recalling the memory of some past indulgence.

Back from the war wiser and ready to run something hot again, Dean started working days at the Urich-Gibb Lincoln-Mercury dealership in Whittier. The war had spun off all kinds of new technologies and parts, and Dean quickly got back into making customized equipment, such as converting Lincoln Zephyr transmissions and ignitions to adapt to Ford V–8 60s. With a head full of hot rod tricks and a group of friends with the best-looking cars in the country, Dean initiated the first hot rod show at the dealership in 1948.

Dean was drafted during the Korean conflict and served in the Air Force as a photographer. This proved to be a lasting benefit in his life, helping him develop his talent for taking sharp photos. He became known as one of the better automotive photojournalists of the early-fifties and started contributing material to two new magazines, *Hot Rod* and *Motor Trend*. Dean continued contributing, on and off, for the next thirty-seven years.

Dean felt his future was in hot rodding. He was still selling his modified components from the back of Moon's Cafe, but eventually he moved to his own shop on South Norwalk Boulevard; he painted it yellow and "Moon Special Equipment" was open.

Business flourished, and he diversified into manifolds, cams, blowers, valve covers, tanks and a vast array of smaller items. His products were the ones to own. He bought out Chuck Potvin Blowers, the makers of crank-mounted superchargers, which is still a regular Moon Equipment product line.

Moon Equipment became an international name in hot rodding. Kings, potentates, scientists, astronauts and police and fire departments called on Dean for extra performance.

Nissan had him build a number of high-performance, small-block Chevrolet racing engines in the sixties for use in one of its racing cars. Dean went with the engines to Japan and oversaw their installation in the Nissan racers at Mt. Fuji Raceway.

Moon Discs, his most unique product, are still sold by the company today. This product was created in the early years of Bonneville and the dry lakes when everyone was trying to find ways of going faster with minimal cost and easy installation. Don Garlits ran them on his streamlined Top Fuel

Moon discs epitomize the cool look on this fuel-injected 1957 Corvette.

dragster in 1986 and 1987 until they were banned by the NHRA for no apparent reason other than sponsor complaints that they covered up the wheel.

Dean's tanks are still hand-spun, as are the discs. Moon Weber manifolds are an industry standard for

Deuce Dante was at the wheel of the "Moonbeam" for the Brighton Speed Trials in England. As usual, the car, and Dean Moon, were smash hits with the British fans.

excellence and are still often seen on high-dollar hot rods.

Moon Equipment is a wonderland of parts and memorabilia. Trophies from his El Mirage days are stacked up, and the office houses a huge collection of items that feature the Moon Eyes logo from the past forty years.

When he moved to the West Coast, Carroll Shelby used Dean's Santa Fe Springs facility to build the first Cobra in sixty days. Dean knew the right connections to make to get the job done; he also knew how to correct the problems that Shelby had with folks out West.

Through the sixties and seventies, Dean continued to run Moon Equipment. He raced a little and played a lot. He raced at Bonneville from the fifties until 1986, when he raced his "Moonbeam" for the last time, continuing to run it with a flathead V–8 60 Ford.

Those who knew Dean knew he could be an endearing man with charm and charisma, and he could be tough and challenging, immediately letting you know his opinion no matter what you thought.

No one ever had a neutral opinion about Dean; you either understood him or you didn't.

Never one to do the "usual," Dean's extensive network of contacts and ear to the ground for the latest gossip made him the listening post for the latest news in the industry. His talents for unusual automotive ideas were sought far and wide, and he appeared in the movies "Eat My Dust," "Hazard Brothers" and "Stroker Ace."

Over the years, the Moon Eyes design became the seventh best-known logo in the world. In college, Dean would type his name and then run the typewriter back and put two commas in the O's. The idea developed further in 1953, when real eyes were painted in the O's on the side of Kreaton Hunter's T roadster drag racer which Moon had sponsored. Finally, in 1957, a Disney commercial artist drew the eyes as they are known today.

Dean enjoyed his notoriety and liked a little comic relief. He is listed several times in the *Guinness Book of World Records*, his favorite entry being for the smallest check, a refund from a courier company for a one-cent overcharge. He worked on several

Dean sits in his famous yellow 1934 roadster, which is powered by a flathead V–8 90. Dale Smith is shown talking with Dean here.

This well-known cartoon was produced when the space race between the United States and the Soviet Union was just heating up. It shows U.S. astronauts discovering just why Dean Moon's ideas and products were considered so far out.

television commercials for Kirin Mets Sodas of Japan. One commercial has him racing down Bonneville only to blow up the engine; stopped in front of a huge billboard of a hand, he is plucked out of the destroyed racer and given a Kirin Mets Soda.

Dean passed away on June 4, 1987. He was one of the toughest men in the industry, but he was also a teacher, a man who freely gave of his knowledge to anyone who was willing to listen.

Throughout his life, his high school sweetheart and wife had always stood with him. Small in stature but big on perception, Shirley Moon stood by this complex man. She was his business partner and together they raised a family of four children. Shirley passed away in late 1989.

Dean was instrumental in the early days of the SEMA, Bonneville Speed Week, the automotive press organizations and magazines and the Southern California Timing Association.

To visit one of the birthplaces of hot rodding, head to 10820 South Norwalk Boulevard in Santa Fe Springs, the location of Moon Equipment. It's as near dead center to the spot as you could likely get. Stand in the yard, close your eyes and dream a little. You'll hear the rumble of a '34 flathead coupe purring through the orange groves.

Chapter 22

Tony Nancy

During part of his career, Tony Nancy was known as "The Loner." It was a catchy, but hardly apt tag for the friendly but quiet master auto craftsman.

Tony wasn't so much a loner as he was an observer and a doer who let his products and his performances speak for him. While other hot rodders and customizers might have been more outspoken and gregarious, Tony was content to simply present his custom work and let the awestruck viewers do the talking.

He enjoyed great success as a drag racer, a custom craftsman, diplomat for American carmakers and racers, stuntman and, fittingly, friend and carmaker for several Hollywood stars.

Tony lived with his mother in California and grew up in Hollywood "going to school and hanging out with the guys." At thirteen, he attended Hollywood High and was crazy about pulling things apart just to see how they worked. "I pulled everything apart: clocks, engines and appliances, and fortunately no one ever yelled at me!" he recalled.

After school and during the summer, Tony worked in Jimmy Summers' Body Shop, sanding and learning the rudiments of paint work, for which he earned twenty-five cents an hour. He was impressionable and thought that any older guy was "to be looked up to, but guys with hot rods were gods." There were numerous race car and auto shops around Los Angeles, and Tony came to know where to go to check out the "right" cars. His first ride into the world of hot rods was a trip to the dry lakes in the back of an eighteen-year-old friend's pickup. He and a buddy rode under a tarp up to El Mirage for a weekend; they slept out, taking in deep breaths of the hot rods and people that came screaming across the lakes. He was hooked: a thirteen-year-old "speed freak."

The following summer, he spent his time at J. N. Brown Upholstery, where he earned "fifty cents an hour and all I could learn." He was ready for his first car. Forty dollars landed him a non-running Model A roadster, and with the help of friends, he got it back on the road.

These were rowdy times for Tony. He was always ready for a street fight and more than once ended up at the local police station. The station sergeant suggested to Tony's mother that he join the Marines to learn a little more self-control. Tony spent three years in the military, including service in Korea in a mine division.

At nineteen, Tony was back on the streets looking for work. His automotive interests and mechanical bent took him back into the upholstery trade, and he worked at Thomas Upholstery, then under the guiding hand of Floyd Owens in Hollywood. Tony learned fine fabric crafting skills that helped him become Hollywood's "Trimmer to the Stars."

Wanting more from a job than Owens could provide, Tony moved to Hillcrest Cadillac, where he took over the upholstery shop. One of Hillcrest's customers was Clark Gable, who had rolled his 1941 Cadillac coupe, which wrinkled the roof but hardly damaged the body. Tony talked Gable into a softly padded California top to cover the damage. The look was a great hit and orders for many others followed.

In the latter part of 1956, Tony opened his own upholstery shop on the corner of Ventura and Woodman in Sherman Oaks, only a block or two from his present shop. Business was quiet at first, but he soon found his niche, fabricating leather interiors for race cars. Tony's dragster and race car interiors would later become a status symbol, and others scrambled to improve the quality of their interiors.

One weekend, a friend took Tony to the San Fernando Drag Races. "I got bit real bad," Tony remembered. "I went home and immediately started on a street roadster." Within months, he was out at San Fernando with his own car. At his first meet, Tony turned 92 mph, winning the street roadster class and collecting the first of thousands of trophies he would win over the next thirty years. His fame grew among the Hollywood set, and Tony crafted more interiors for Clark Gable and Gary Cooper, as well as a trick interior for Lance Reventlow's Mercedes 300SL.

His business developed and Tony started racing his roadster as often as possible. Kent Fuller, a promising young chassis builder, built the roadster chassis while a tenant of Tony's shop. Tony had picked the number twenty-two as his race number, and the junior title came from the junior-sized motor. As such, "22 Jr." was born, a title that would stick to the last day he raced. Tony was not just the driver. He would also wrench on the motor and do all the suspension work. The roadster was powered by a 238 destroked flathead.

His success with the first roadster led to his building a second one, which put Tony on the cover of *Hot Rod* magazine. This roadster was powered by an injected Buick. It had a Kent Fuller chassis and ran 138 mph on gas. Four roadsters passed through Tony's shop before he moved into dragsters. Tony became known for the quality of his cars as much as for his on-track performances, which are recorded with *Hot Rod* magazine covers in 1962, 1963, 1964 and 1967.

In 1961, Tony built a new, modified A/MR Roadster. Fuller did the chassis work, and it was powered by a blown gas Buick. At the 1962 Winternationals, Tony ran 169 mph for a new class record. This beautiful, red, 1927 T roadster-body dragster was finely-detailed and, of course, had the full Tony Nancy interior.

Tony started his most famous racer, the silver 22 Jr., in 1963. It set a new standard for body, paint,

Tony is looking clean-cut and handsome with his silver, front-engined dragster.

Tony wins another first place and gets to pose with the trophy girl.

engineering and performance. Fuller fabricated the chassis, but this time, it was a hand-formed alloy body designed by Steve Swaja and hammered out by Emil Diedt at L.A. Metal Shaping. The body featured an enclosed chute pack and a finely tapered nose.

At the 1963 Winternationals, Tony cleaned up in his class, with 164.83 mph at 8.97 seconds for the

Tony blasts it down the track in his 22 Jr. '29 roadster riding on '32 rails.

AA/C division title. 22 Jr. was powered by a blown-gas Dodge "wedge head" and was sponsored by Plymouth. Tony also won the "Best Engineered" award at the 1963 Winternationals.

During these years, Tony took his cars on extensive tours across the country, racing both bracket and match events. He picked up the handle of "The Loner" from an ex-girlfriend who complained that he never needed any help. Tony drove from track to track and found someone to work as his pit crew at each event. His cars were always immaculate and well-prepared.

He was famous as a drag racer, but the best was yet to come. He toured Italy and England after he built the first of his new "Wedge" series of rear-engined dragsters. This dragster was hauled off to Europe and toured with Don Garlits, delighting the crowds at each stop.

The Wedge was both revolutionary and evolutionary. The front-engined "slingshot" dragster had dominated since the beginning of drag racing, but with the Wedge, Tony opened a new vista of design. Not only was the engine behind the driver, but it had a fully enclosed body and limited rear suspension. The Wedge was powered by a 427-ci blown Plymouth "Wedge" motor. The motor was bored and stroked out to 486 ci and used Enderle fuel injection. With Wedge I, Tony became the first gas/blown car into the six-second bracket, and it won its class at the 1964 Winternationals.

The Wedge met with considerable success and became the most famous dragster of its time. As with all Nancy race cars, the Wedge had a perfect Scotch glove leather interior, which was carefully crafted to suit Tony's build.

Even though Tony had developed an international reputation in drag racing he still tried to keep his shop running back in Hollywood.

On tour across the country, he had a few startling crashes. While racing Garlits at the old Sandusky strip in Ohio, Tony went through the traps backwards at 180 mph when one of the friction shocks in the rear suspension collapsed and "corked" the car.

Wedge II was built a year later. In Italy on the straightaway of the Monza track, Tony ran 196 mph with the new Oldsmobile-powered Wedge II.

The title of "The Loner" was a fine professional tag but it didn't fit Tony's personality. He had developed a large circle of close friends from many walks of life. "I discovered that automobiles crossed all boundaries: language, race, place, money or no money. The car was common ground for anyone. I have friends in all parts of the world, and I get mail from people I've never heard of because we all have one interest in common: fast cars."

This connection with fast cars brought many of Hollywood's stars into Tony's life. Steve McQueen was a regular late-night caller at the shop as well as a

*Tony sits in his perfect 1929 A roadster outside his shop in
Sherman Oaks.*

*Tony works out his positioning ahead of the mock engine
while laying out the Maxi-Wedge.*

The famous Plymouth Wedge dragster took Tony to fame and fortune around the world.

weekend bike racing buddy, and they became close friends. McQueen asked Tony to take over the management of his Solar Plastics Company. He needed someone he could trust who knew how to get a job done properly. Tony didn't want to change occupations but decided to help out. He got the company out of its hole and onto its feet, making rotation-molded motorcycle parts for Montgomery Ward. Tony liked the idea and worked on developing the polyethylene lightweight seat and fuel cell, both of which are common today. He continued to race while working at Solar and even started doing some off-road work.

Tony spent his quarter-mile time handling his rambunctious Olds-powered rear-motor car. It was in the top gas class, but the Oldsmobile motors were not able to take the punishment. Tony remembered,

"We were forever putting broken motors together, so I gave it away as a bad deal." Tony raced for McQueen in the 1968 Baja 1,000, taking Don Prud-homme along as co-pilot. He left Solar eighteen months later, to become his own boss again.

Tony landed TV contracts not as a drag racer or trimmer but as a full-fledged stuntman. Since the late-sixties, he has done numerous stunts for the

Tony "explodes" during this run at Pomona.

Tony was always the center of attraction at any event.

movies, including "Honky Tonk Freeway," "Holly-wood Knights" and "Morro." He now does more TV than film and serves as stunt coordinator for the Action Driving Team.

Back in the upholstery business after leaving Solar, Tony continued to build his reputation as "The Master of the Trade." He continued to use his sea horse logo, which was the identification for all his work. He developed special techniques for stitching boat interiors and reintroduced some old ways of getting an upholstery job done to perfection. He did fewer jobs and charged more for the ones he did take on, which allowed him to do his work as he chose.

Tony was thinking about getting into fuel racing when his old buddy Prudhomme "shamed me into building a new car," Tony recalled. Using a de-stroked Keith Black Hemi, Tony broke 228 mph at Bakersfield, with Prudhomme wrenching the motor for him; at Lions, he went 230 mph. Tony won the 1970 U.S. Fuel and Gas Championships, beating nearly 200 of the world's fastest cars with a time of 236 mph.

His next dragster was his first Top Fuel car. He built it in 1972 and was among the first to use wings as aerodynamic aids. Tony installed a set of Don Long-designed canard winglets in front of the tires to get the air moving over them, and a wing over the front axle to help keep it on the ground. This car became the famous "Wynns Sizzler," AA/FD rail. It sat on a 220-in. wheelbase and was powered by a Keith Black 426 blown Hemi. This car raced against the best, including Ivo, Garlits, McEwen and Prud-homme.

Tony went to Japan under contract with Wynns and a Japanese company to do a promotional tour. The Wynns Sizzler was air-freighted to Japan at a cost of $21,000. The trip was an enjoyable and funny time for Tony. At the Mt. Fuji Raceway 115,000 people who saw him do a fire burnout lept to their feet, screaming. According to Tony, the burnout also "frightened the livin' daylights out of the fire mar-shals at the track," who responded by attempting to extinguish the burnout as Tony left the water trough and smoked it out through the timing lights.

He still had the need for speed. In 1976, he went to Bonneville and broke 200 mph in the Leggit Lakester, and he met the late Garry Gabelich. Gabe-lich wanted Tony to do a stunt with him, which would involve Gabelich holding onto the push bar of Tony's dragster while wearing a set of roller skates. Tony would leave the traps in his usual manner, with

Tony's latest project is a ZR-1-powered custom 1940 Ford convertible.

Gabelich holding on. Gabelich would let go by releasing a 'chute on his back and pulling away from the dragster. Tony considered it but declined.

By this time, Tony had won both the U.S. Fuel and Gas Championship, the All-Pro Series and had been NHRA World Champion, but he wasn't quite finished. His last car was another Top Fuel racer known as the "Revell-Liner." This bright yellow car won plenty of meets but had never proved itself as a highly competitive racer.

Tony toured Australia with the car, and enjoyed the difference in cultures, but was starting to feel the pressure of professional drag racing. He could see the writing on the wall. "Ten top teams and a handful of also-rans," Tony recalled, "I didn't want to be an also-ran, and being one of the select few was more work than I wanted. Yet, when I finally quit in 1980, I felt such a low in my life. It was not the glory, but the excitement, the smell of the fuel and the burning odor of rubber, which can still get the hairs on my arm to stand up. I realize that it's all a period of my life which has passed, and that's OK. I am in the shop now doing my trimming, but I sure miss the narcotic effect of driving one of those big cars."

Tony still works out in his own gym and keeps an immaculate shop where he does some of the finest interior work this side of Italy. He is also building an ultra-cool 1939 Ford convertible powered by a ZR–1 Corvette motor.

Not only was Tony a perfectionist with his cars and his driving, but his talent with the needle and thread is renowned throughout the world of high-dollar exotics and hot rodding. A Tony Nancy interior rates with a Keith Black motor, a Brizio chassis, Coddington wheels and paint from Junior's House of Color.

Tony still has a solid, well-built, suntanned California look about him. His youthfulness overflows as he talks about his latest commercial ventures. He has just started hosting the TV series "Concours Automotive Video." He also has released a series of special car-care products for leather interiors and aftermarket accessories for Chevy Blazers.

The man with the sea horses still enjoys drag racing, but the best of times were when he was at the wheel. "There is nothing on earth like the surge of power that a Top Fuel car delivers through your body, running out the 'back door.' What a ride."

Chapter 23

Wally Parks

There is a great romantic appeal to hot rodding, especially to its early days, which were wild and lustful, with lots of young men souping up and customizing cars to give them their own identities so the young men could make their marks just as distinctly.

Hot rodding might never have progressed beyond those wild and lustful days of street racing if not for Wally Parks, a man who recognized the sport's potential to become an acceptable part of American automotive history and culture.

Parks' efforts and commitment helped carry hot rodding from the California dry lakes of the thirties to prime-time television in the eighties. He was one of the founders and a long-time president of the National Hot Rod Association (NHRA), one of the most valuable and influential organizations in the

automotive world. Wally was born in Goltry, Oklahoma. His family moved west to the warmth of California. His father, a carpenter by trade, sold the family possessions, stacked the remains onto a Ford Model T touring car and then headed west with three children, a wife and a grandmother to join his brother in Santa Ana.

As a child, automobiles fascinated Wally—especially race cars—but they were uncommon, so Wally sought them out. In doing so, he discovered Eddie and Lou Meyer's shop, where he could peek inside and check out "wild and interesting racing devices."

Every week, he and his buddies scraped together twenty-five cents to get a ticket to the infield at old Ascot raceway in Alhambra. Even when they

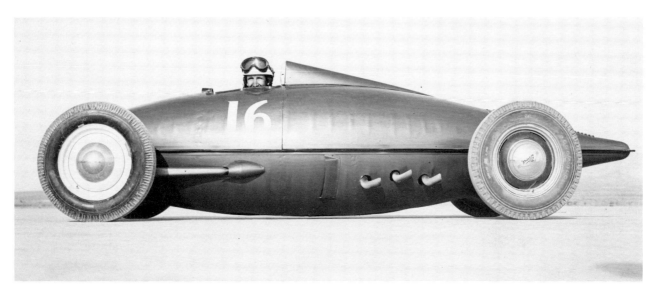

Wally in the "Burkes Tank" at the dry lakes. Dean Moon

Wally in the backyard with one of his first "racers" in the thirties.

couldn't get the cash together, they would ride the street cars up to the track and watch the races from a hill overlooking the track.

He spent his high school years at Davis Star Jordan High School in Watts. He was among the first students to be bused to high school to promote racial integration. Wally recalled that, "At the time, it didn't seem like anything different. I had friends in every different cultural group. Those friendships have served me well, as they gave me a better grasp of people in general."

Weekends had him racing "push carts" with his friends along the dusty streets of South Gate and playing competitive sports against another neighborhood team.

The high school auto shop further tantalized Wally's interest in automobiles. The shop had a T roadster which was to be stripped and rebuilt as a class project, but Wally was in drafting and art classes. "Somehow, I always managed to drift in and out of the auto shop while my classes were going on," Wally recalled. Those days were an enjoyable time for him. He walked home with Glen Seaborg, a bright, promising student who would eventually become head of the Atomic Energy Commission. Family life was secure and happy with a family of four children and a new home that his father and two brothers had built.

Wally worked at his uncle's hardware store on weekends. He was looking for a car, and another uncle offered him one in exchange for four weekends of yard work. Wally completed his side of the deal and got the car, a 1924 Chevrolet Touring car, a few weeks later.

What better daily transportation than a 1932 Ford roadster for the editor of Hot Rod *magazine in the late fifties.*

136

He was ready with his first modification. Off came the muffler and on went a three-foot section of brass pipe from a Simmons bed. Wally still did not have a license, so the Chevy was limited to the short driveway and back-streets. The day he turned sixteen, he was off, but not for long. Two blocks was all it took to end the days of the Chevy. The steering linkage dropped off just as he reached 20 mph. Unfortunately, parked on the side of the street was a new maroon Essex with a proud new owner at the wheel. With Wally unable to stop, the Chevy took a slow turn smack into the Essex, cowpunching the left front fender. Wally had to sell his Chevy to pay for the damage to the Essex, and he was back on his bike for local transportation.

A year later, he found his first roadster. It was for sale, without tires, for $4. He borrowed a set of tires, drove it home and rebuilt the engine several times, learning more each time about the internal workings and the external relationship of the engine's components. It was to be the first of many Fords that Wally would own.

He graduated from high school and took a job with a local laundry as a delivery man. He loved the job because it gave him his own 1929 Ford Model A delivery panel truck. Wally laughingly referred to himself as the "first hot rod laundry delivery man, and I was always on time."

One weekend in 1933, Wally and friends drove up to the dry lakes. They had heard about the hot rodders racing there and wanted to see the action for themselves. Forty miles short of Muroc, they broke the ring gear on their Model T coupe but ventured on, hitching a ride to the races.

There were about seventy cars racing. "Wild and wonderful hot rods" were blasting down the dry dirt lake. Without a car, the guys walked up and down the lake watching the races. The course had a three-mile acceleration zone, followed by a one-mile timing trap. Wally was entranced.

The organizers, the Muroc Timing Association, were short of helpers and asked for volunteers to help run the event. Wally volunteered to man an observation post halfway down the course, using a party line telephone in the back of a dump truck to report on the competitors as they ran down the track.

Wally loved the atmosphere of the racing and the people involved. Soon, he was back with a fenderless Ford roadster and in June 1933, he turned 82.19 mph on the lakes. With his new interest in hot

Wally at Daytona Speed Week with the Hot Rod *magazine special.* Dean Moon

The Hot Rod *magazine special at Daytona. Wally got a two-way average of 159.89 mph in 1960. Later that year,* with a Moon-built engine, Ray Brock pulled 183 mph. Dean Moon

rods and his talent for organizing, Wally helped the California Roadrunners Club, a hot rod club still active today.

Wally changed jobs and worked on the General Motors Corporation production line in South Gate as a "nut runner," assembling Pontiacs, Oldsmobiles and Buicks. It didn't take long for him to move up the ladder and become a test driver, which pleased him greatly. He could go back to his old joy of driving.

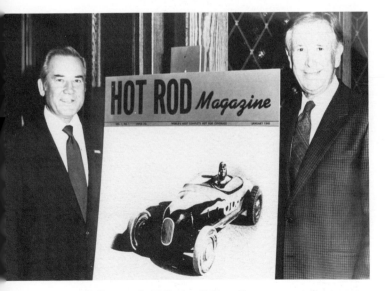

Wally, on the right, with Pete Petersen at a dinner commemorating Hot Rod *magazine.*

By 1939, the lakes had become a hot bed of racing activity, but there was no organizing body to oversee all the groups that wanted to use the dry lakes. The Southern California Timing Association (SCTA) was formed to act as a cover group for about twenty hot rod clubs that regularly used the lakes. Two representatives were sent from each club to form the SCTA.

This new group was set to handle the running of dry lakes events and to deal with legal matters, should they crop up from time to time.

World War II closed down the domestic automobile production at South Gate and the factory was turned over to light tank production. Wally had begun sketching "unflattering cartoons of management" for his local union newspaper. The head of the plant needed a production illustrator, so Wally was shipped off to the arts center for a rapid course in production artwork and illustration. Back at the plant, he produced assembly diagrams and manuals for production line workers.

With that project complete, he asked to be transferred back to the testing unit, where he spent twelve months as a test driver of M5-A1 light-armored tanks. He enlisted, was trained and sent out as a technical sergeant in the 754th Tank Battalion. Wally had his own tank retriever and fought in the Philippines, Bougainville and the other Solomon Islands. Even in the islands, his hot rod fever did not subside. He built his own "hot rod Jeep" by scavenging parts from various sources. The result was a two-wheel-drive Jeep powered by a Ford V-8 60, which he and a few dry lakes buddies used to terrorize officers on small back roads.

Out of the service, Wally returned to GM as an illustrator, but his interest in hot rodding continued. He became president of the SCTA in 1946 and then moved into a full-time position as its general manager in 1947. That was a crucial year for hot rodding and it was young Wally Parks and publicist Robert "Pete" Petersen who battled with the press and police for the sport's rights.

Wally and Petersen joined forces through a phone conversation. Petersen was with Hollywood Publicity Associates, where he helped organize publicity for auto shows. At that time there was public and police pressure "to make hot rods illegal on public highways." Wally remembered that, "Pete saw the looming hot rod debate as a public relations problem and [said] that Hollywood Publicity Associates could help to deal with them."

Money was a problem, and they needed to raise funds for the lobbying effort they were about to undertake. Wally suggested a hot rod show and Petersen liked the idea. Wally had the resources to put together a show with his SCTA members and their rods. Petersen handled publicity and promotion and collected some Hollywood stars to act as draws to the show.

Wally recalled that, "The show was to demonstrate the nature of hot rodding to the public that the media was not painting, and hopefully get an effective publicity campaign going to counter the impending hot rod legislation."

The result was the 1947 Los Angeles Hot Rod Show at the Armory. Ten-thousand people turned up. Radio and TV loved the show and the newspapers all gave it the good coverage the SCTA was seeking. The show's great success had several effects, the most noticeable of which was that it triggered Petersen to change his career the following year and become a magazine publisher.

Wally did not sit still either. Within a year, he had become the editor of Petersen's *Hot Rod* magazine and president of the National Hot Rod Association (NHRA) which Petersen helped him form. Using *Hot Rod* magazine as a platform, Wally spent the next fifteen years working both jobs. He eventually resigned as editor of the magazine to become full-time president of the NHRA.

Wally can be described as the man responsible for modern-day drag racing. As part of his activities at Trend Publishing, he worked on a series of *Motor Trend/Hot Rod* magazine car evaluations. They were carried out on a section of the abandoned Ramona airport. Wally had a Lincoln to test, and the quarter-mile track was selected after the group found that if they accelerated for more than a quarter-mile, the Lincoln had trouble stopping on what was left of the runway!

The day turned into the first match race. Fred Davies, a San Diego auto dealer who was on hand after hearing that "a few cars would be running at Ramona airport" drove a new Oldsmobile 88. He paired it off against the clock with many of the other cars, and match racing was born the same day as the quarter-mile.

Wally's work with the magazines in 1949 eventually led the newly formed NHRA to choose the quarter-mile as the official track distance. In his position as editor, Wally helped give hot rodding a new image. He had become drag racing's spokesperson.

As part of dry lakes-SCTA management, Wally, Ak Miller, Petersen and Lee Ryan traveled to Salt Lake City in 1947 to seek permission to use the Bonneville Salt Flats for speed trials. They received a favorable response, and in 1949, the first Bonneville Speed Week was held. Wally led the planning and helped set up the track. He returned the following year as an organizer and racer, driving the Burke/Francisco Tank, powered by a fuel-injected flathead, to 148 mph.

Once, on a trip through the Midwest, Wally and Don Francisco, one of *Hot Rod*'s technical writers, pulled into a gas station. The kid pumping gas was

Wally, president of the National Hot Rod Association.

beside himself because right there, in his station were the editor of *Hot Rod*, the *Hot Rod* Tank and pull car, and Don Francisco. Inside the shop, Francisco and Wally found a V–8 60 upside down on a stool, half-assembled. Propped up beside it was a copy of *Hot Rod* with a Francisco feature on how to build a hot V–8 60. The kid was building the engine right out of the magazine! Wally and Francisco were reminded of the incredible impact they had on rodders everywhere.

These were exciting times. Quarter-mile strips flowered overnight along the West Coast. "Pappy" Hart opened Santa Ana Drags in 1950 after seeing the potential of drag racing that first day at Ramona.

It seemed that Wally somehow cloned himself into half a dozen people during the next five years because he was involved in so much raw history of the sport. It's hard to believe he ever slept. In its formative years, the NHRA benefited from his experience with the SCTA. Using the basics of the dry lakes rules and getting an insurance rider from a

Wally (right) chats with fellow hot rod legend Tom Medley.

140

Chicago circle track group allowed him to get the ball rolling. Petersen chipped in $1,100 to get the NHRA off the ground and helped out when the organization floundered three times before it took up the challenge to become the master of organized drag racing.

It took several years before the socially oriented NHRA would look at drag racing as a piece of its turf. Actually, only three years later, it staged the first Southern California Championship Drags, for which 15,000 people turned up in Pomona. Chief Parker of the Los Angeles Police Department was on hand for the first event and endorsed it as "a civic service that encourages safety and helps with the enforcement of the law."

It turned out to be the pivotal point for the NHRA. The association had been a semi-social car club, not an association of racers, but Wally liked what he saw in drag racing, and the association took a new direction. The need to promote drag racing as a safe sport was obvious to Wally and with a crew of three, he set out on a national educational tour in 1954, the first Safety Safari.

Headed up by Bud Coons, the Safety Safari traveled around the country with a trailer containing a full Chrondek timing outfit and other equipment for setting up a drag strip. Living on a shoestring budget, the Safety Safari showed not only the police and city councils but also hot rodders the benefits and mechanics of organizing and running a quarter-mile drag strip.

The successes of the NHRA in the early-fifties led to its first national event, a double-header scheduled for September 29, 1955 at the airport in Great Bend, Kansas. The three-day event got off to a dry start on Friday, but overnight rain turned it into an unrunnable event, with six inches of water covering the drag strip. The event was cancelled on Saturday morning and rescheduled in Phoenix, Arizona, six weeks later.

Continuing his work as *Hot Rod* editor, Wally helped develop *Hot Rod*'s place in the history books of American publishing. Wally had a great feel for what the readers wanted and how it should be presented to them; he wanted the reader to be able to relate directly to what his magazine was saying.

He also drove in the famous Daytona Beach Time Trials with a 1957 Plymouth Savoy hardtop. He took his technical editor and the next *Hot Rod* editor, Ray Brock, along. They used an alcohol fuel Hemi fitted with water injection for Daytona and managed, after much wrangling with the NASCAR people, to finally get a run on the last afternoon of the week. The Plymouth ran 161 mph. They went to Bonneville in 1958 and ran 200 mph with the same car.

Wearing two hats became increasingly difficult, and Wally finally resigned as editor of *Hot Rod* to become the full-time president of the NHRA. In some ways, it slowed the progress of the association because Wally no longer had direct access to the drag racing hot rodders that *Hot Rod* offered, but the close cooperation did continue for many years.

By the mid-sixties, drag racing had developed into a large, spectator sport, and Wally managed to get broad coverage from the television networks. The NHRA finally got its finances together and when major sponsors moved into the sport, the association never looked back.

Under Wally's guidance, the NHRA bought Indianapolis Raceway Park and turned it into one of the best multi-motorsport complexes in the country, with SCCA, NASCAR and the NHRA using the facility. Gainesville, Florida, was next on the list, along with the leasing of Pomona in Los Angeles, and Bakersfield.

Wally insisted that all of these accomplishments were not his alone. His wife Barbara, for example, worked diligently by his side, running various facets of the NHRA and helping him focus on the needs of the association. One of her major contributions was the development of the new tower and track facilities at Indianapolis Raceway Park.

Wally still has a number of interesting projects he wants to translate into reality. He would like the NHRA to re-develop some of its long-lost roots, and he wants "more hot rodding" involvement. He has moved to develop an educational program and is working to open up other new areas under the NHRA umbrella.

The sport of hot rodding would not have climbed out of its anti-social street-racing roots so easily if Wally Parks had not had the motivation and vision of a progressive hot rod future. He championed the cause, planted the seeds, watered the crop and is reaping the rewards of a life dedicated to the sport of hot rodding.

Chapter 24

Robert E. "Pete" Petersen

The world of hot rodding owes a great deal to Pete Petersen. Without his motivation and contributions, the sport might have withered and died on the vine. Certainly, it would never have enjoyed its incredible worldwide popularity without his spreading the good word from the birthplace of the sport, California. He became a catalyst who helped hot rodding develop and mature from an outlaw pursuit to a

The custom-flamed Ford panel truck which Hot Rod *used to cover such events as Bonneville. Left to right: Wally* Parks, Floyd Wheeler and Pete Petersen. Petersen Photo Library

socially-accepted pastime. The millions of enthusiasts around the world who enjoy hot rodding today might never have been exposed to the sport, its cars, legends and mileposts, if not for the work of Pete Peterson.

Pete was a bright young man with a strong Danish background who spent his early years in Barstow, California, where he pumped gas after school and on weekends. At the station, he saw the hot rodders heading for the dry lakes. It looked like an interesting pastime, but it would be years before he had a hot rod of his own. He entered Army Special Training at the end of high school and spent several years learning its disciplines.

In the mid-forties, he moved to Los Angeles to look for work. He found a messenger job at MGM and worked his way into the publicity department. Unfortunately, MGM was having difficult financial times just after the war and had to lay off Pete and a large section of the public relations department. But his former co-workers founded a new cooperative public relations company called "Hollywood Publicity Associates" and invited him to join them.

The group was about twenty-seven members strong, all ex-MGM employees. They handled everything from the Hap Well football team to automotive events. Pete's responsibility was "Mad Man Muntz" and his sports car account.

The dry lakes were booming and street racing around Los Angeles was at its height, but the police, local PTAs and city council were concerned about the street activities.

Pete thought this might cause the sport considerable trouble, so he called Wally Parks of the Southern California Timing Association. It was the beginning of a lifetime friendship. Parks told Pete that, "Yes, he needed good PR but had no money." Parks did, however, have an idea for a car show that could produce some money and Pete loved it. Colonel Mike Lynch of the Greater Los Angeles Safety Council was pressing for a ban on all forms of motorsports. His attempt to end all racing united many folks and sparked an immediate call for positive publicity for hot rodding.

The spin-off of all the negative publicity was the golden opportunity Pete and Parks were waiting for. With the approval of the L.A. police and the help of many groups, a hot rod show was held in the Los Angeles Armory. It showed the public that hot rodding was more than just the wild street racing the press had depicted. The show attracted a huge amount of excellent press, radio and TV coverage.

The event was so successful that the L.A. chapter of the National Safety Council backed down on its anti-hot rodding campaign and even allowed the SCTA to become one of its members.

With Bob Lindsay as his partner, Pete formed a company to publish a magazine for hot rodders. Lindsay's father was in the publishing business with a

magazine called *Tail Wagger,* and provided many contacts to help get the new magazine off the ground.

Pete managed to scramble together $400 for his part of the printing. The first printing of 10,000 copies was rushed off a press in the basement of the Page Military Camp and introduced at the Armory show as *Hot Rod* magazine. It sold out at twenty-five cents a copy.

The early issues were sold at hot rod gatherings, and subscriptions were collected at these events and from dealers. Pete hit the street to sign up dealers in Los Angeles, selling single copies to passers-by and taking subscriptions at every opportunity. Lindsay organized the editorial materials, dealt with advertisers and gave the magazine its direction.

It was produced in a one-room office on South La Brea, with only a desk, a typewriter and a couple of pairs of hands. There was no telephone and many times Pete slept in the office.

The early issues included not only California hot rodding news but also historical stories, stories about racing in Indiana, custom cars, the dry lakes and performance modification features. It was a new style of *Popular Mechanics*, dedicated exclusively to hot rodding.

HOT ROD OF THE MONTH

Sitting in the driver's seat is Eddie Hulse, who, a few moments after this picture was taken, drove number 668, to set a new SCTA record for Class C roadsters. Hulse, a native Californian, nosed out Randy Shinn, a long-time top honor holder for the RC Class. Shinn's old record was 129.40 in a channeled Mercury T.

Keeping the Car Out Front by George Riley—Page 10

The cover of the first Hot Rod *magazine, January 1948. The price was twenty-five cents, and the first cover boy was Eddie Hulse in his record-setting Class C roadster.*

Hot Rod and the NHRA-sponsored this streamliner in 1953 at Bonneville Speed Week. Petersen Photo Library

Pete shooting photos for an early edition of Hot Rod *magazine on the Southern California Dry Lakes.* Petersen Photo Library

Both Petersen and Lindsay spent a good deal of time selling subscriptions and collecting information for the first issues. "Photos by Pete" became a famous catch phrase as Pete honed his photography skills in between selling copies and mingling with potential advertisers at the lakes, shows and drags.

The small staff became a strong editorial team after the first few issues. Tom Medley was the resident humorist and eventually became editor of *Hot Rod* and other Petersen magazines.

The magazines grew by leaps and bounds. The need to sell individual copies on the street diminished when a contract for wholesale distribution was signed. Walt Woron was the magazine's first acting editor in 1949 but within a year, Pete had appointed Parks as *Hot Rod*'s first full-time editor. 1950 was a year of change: Lindsay left the company and Pete took complete control as publisher.

Slowly, he built a solid financial base. The term "hot rod" still had not become socially acceptable, and many of Pete's associates felt that the name of the magazine should be changed, but Pete stayed with the title. By the mid-fifties, *Hot Rod* had grown into a sizeable publication with a circulation of 400,000. Advertisers quickly realized that the magazine was a direct line to every teenager who had an interest in anything automotive. Over the next fif-

The custom-built camera car which Hot Rod *magazine used to shoot photos of Bonneville Speed Week in 1951, with Tom Medley driving.* Petersen Photo Library

"The Hot Rod Speed Wagon." Petersen Photo Library

teen years, circulation continued to rise; it peaked at more than a million copies monthly.

Pete's interest in hot rodding went far deeper than just another commercial venture. With Parks and Ryan, he convinced the Utah Chamber of Commerce to grant permission to use Bonneville Salt Flats as a location for "all-out racing." *Hot Rod* co-sponsored the first Bonneville Speed Week. The "sport of speed" had turned another corner in its long road to popular acceptance, and Speed Week continues to be hot rodding's premier event.

The selection of editor has always been important to Pete and only the very best of hot rodding's automotive writers have made it onto the masthead:

Pete smiles from the center of twenty years of Hot Rod *magazine.* Petersen Photo Library

146

Ray Brock, Jim McFarland, John Dianna, Lee Kelly, Jim McGraw, Terry Cook and Leonard Emanuelson have been some of "the chosen few."

Petersen Publishing flourished because of *Hot Rod*, and other automotive magazines followed, including *Motor Trend, Car Craft,* and *Rod and Custom*. Sports, photography, hunting, fishing, trucks and watersports magazines have also helped build Petersen Publishing into one of America's great publishing success stories.

Pete also helped the company's financial base by developing many real estate holdings, but is still involved with the everyday running of Petersen Publishing.

He is known for his sportsmanship and travels the world in search of select hunting grounds and great fishing. His interest in the automotive world continues and he has an extensive car collection, including a selection of hot rods.

Pete's dream to start a magazine was simple enough, but never imagined that "the boy from Barstow" would build one of America's most respected magazine publishing houses. His determination to do his very best has enriched all readers' lives. *Hot Rod* magazine continues to be the most-read automotive magazine in the world. It has been read, shared and collected by three generations, a rare compliment that ranks it with *National Geographic* as a valued source of information and inspiration.

Robert E. "Pete" Petersen, the founder of Hot Rod *magazine.* Petersen Photo Library

Chapter 25

Ed Roth

You can rest assured that "Big Daddy" Ed Roth didn't get invited to many PTA meetings in the sixties.

No, Ed was not popular with some of the more straight-laced and tradition-bound folks who took great umbrage with his outrageous T-shirts.

Ed not only changed the look of the cars he customized in spectacular but sometimes outrageous fashion, he also changed the way America's youth

One of Ed's publicity photos for his line of "Rat Fink" wares.

and hot rodders dressed. Instead of wearing standard-issue white T-shirts or shirts with a simple "Sta-Lube" logo on the pocket, young men and Big Daddy loyalists took to wearing shirts with crowd-stopping characters like Davey, Mother's Worry and the great Rat Fink.

Don't blame (or among hot rodders, credit) Big Daddy for generating the wild characters and images all by himself. It turns out that when he started giving rodders a taste of his madness, they loved it so much that they egged him on and demanded that he get more and more outrageous. "The wilder, the better," was the way Ed's fans have viewed his works.

In the early-fifties, Ed was asked to draw the logo for the Drag Wagons Car Club of Maywood, California sweatshirts. At Ed's suggestion, he also did a caricature of each member on the member's jacket. Each member wanted something distinct, so he gave them bug eyes and broken teeth and had them picking their noses. Incredibly, that turned out to be exactly what they wanted.

Ed had created his own monster, starting a fashion trend with hot rod cartooning. At first he used felt pens, then an air pencil, which was unheard of in the early-fifties. (The air pencil was an early version of the airbrush and was used as a commercial cake-decorating tool.)

Ed grew up in southern California and by age fifteen, he was running a 1933 Ford coupe at the Clock Drive-In. He gathered with the likes of Dean Moon, Vic Edelbrock and the Chrisman brothers to talk cars, do some cruising and drag race. Over the years, his cars read like "Who's Who of Hot Rodding": a '39 Chevy, 1946 Ford, Henry J, 1930 Ford. And they had components like Olds motors and transmissions, chopped tops and sectioned bodies.

148

This was Ed's homework. He was not a student of books but was a natural with his hands. Ed followed the design philosophy of Dr. Porsche: Give the people what they need, not what they want. Make it look good as well as make it work. And keep it simple.

Ed dislikes the way students at today's arts centers are taught to design what he considers ugly, overweight castings and stampings on American cars, "Arts Center Phobia," he calls it, "the loss of individuality and free form that has hit current design concepts and has stifled them by making them conform to what is expected." As Ed said, "Where would I have been in the fifties if I'd had to conform to the arts center?" Today, he is a guest lecturer at an L.A. area art center. With free thinking and a free hand to produce works based on his own concepts, whatever they may have been, Ed's art became a design category set well apart from the mainstream.

Drag racing on Slauson Avenue in the forties; chopping and channeling Deuce coupes; sustaining hundreds of cuts and bruises from tools, grinders, nuts and bolts; building and grinding fiberglass, then driving the finished product: this was Ed's arts center. His ability to visualize was his greatest strength.

An Air Force stint as a cartographer took Ed into the depths of the Sahara Desert near Casablanca, where he worked on top-secret projects doing highly technical aero-reconnaissance mapping to accurate-

Ed with "Road Agent."

ly track the flight of Soviet and English aircraft, as well as UFOs. (You may not believe in UFOs, but he does.)

The technical drafting skill he learned in the desert helped him develop his talent to draw, do caricatures and design. Yet, he remained independent and creative. When his buddies were drinking

"Beatnik Bandit," Ed's most famous hot rod.

and womanizing, spending their money, Ed was dreaming of carb set-ups and welding equipment. He read voraciously, especially about automotive topics.

One story caught his eye: a photo of Henry Ford pounding the trunk of a 1941 sedan with a sledge-hammer. Amazingly, the trunk was undented; it was made out of fiberglass. Ed was impressed and thought at the time, "That's my kind of stuff." Immediately upon his return to California, he found a fiberglass supplier. He bought enough to try it out, but his first adventure was a catastrophe. It ran all over his clothes, hardened his shoes and left big lumps on the driveway, but it convinced him he could build a fiberglass car!

With a head full of ideas, the latest technology and the necessary skills, he made his first products. He then cut them up, started over and modified them. The sculptor had found his medium. Ed was the first sculptor of the modern age to make functional, road-going designs in the way traditional sculpture was crafted. This was the key to Ed's success and the prime motivator of the hot rod idea of building true one-off custom rods.

By 1961, Ed was on the show trail with a new custom car to exhibit as a promotional attraction for his expanding T-shirt business. Ed was the leader in airbrushed T-shirts at hot rod shows. The cost for an original Roth T-shirt was $1.50—compared to $35 now.

"Beatnik Bandit," Ed's most famous show car, is a prime example of his talent with plaster and glass. The idea came from a discussion about "the ultimate rod" one afternoon with Joe Henning of *Hot Rod* magazine. Ed was so stimulated by the ideas they discussed that he went straight home, got out the plaster and started working on his new rod.

Weeks later, with a five-foot-high "mistake pile," Ed had the Bandit finished and ready for glass. He bought a 1949 Oldsmobile chassis and running gear, and shortened the chassis considerably (by about five feet). He gave the Olds ohv engine the classic hot rod look with a GMC blower, twin Ford carbs and a total chrome finish on nearly everything. He decked the interior in white Naugahyde with deep padding to give it a classy, comfortable look.

Ed fitted the Bandit with a unique single-control stick operating the turning, throttle and braking. In the late-fifties in the army surplus stores, Ed found all kinds of pumps and hydraulic rams he used to build Bandit's control system. The paint scheme featured white pearlescence with gold and brown-tone panels mixed with black and white matching stripes.

Ed back in the "Bad Old Days," as he calls them.

Ed finishing off one of his many "Rat Fink" cars. He stopped building them when he discovered that they frightened children.

The bubble top was made in a pizza oven as a one-off item, using compressed air to inflate the sheet of clear acrylic plastic into a dome. This car was built at the height of the Beatnik era and when Ed saw a newspaper headline "Beatnik Bandit Robs Store," he named the car "Beatnik Bandit."

Ed was big news by this time with both the kids and adults; you either loved his radical designs or you hated what he stood for. It was hip to wear a Roth T-shirt: "Mother's Worry," "Lonesome," "Rat Fink." They were cool and very funny. Yet at the time, these T-shirts were seen as the ruination of young men's minds.

More than twenty-five years later, those designs have enjoyed a resurgence of popularity. Ed hits the summer show circuit to do customized one-off T-shirts and sell his standard line of shirts. "Rat Fink," his most famous T-shirt design, was conceived on a napkin in a restaurant one night as Ed entertained a friend with a crazy story about what Mickey Mouse's father would look like. Today, Rat Fink has his own club, "Rat Finks of America," with pins and an annual party.

When Beatnik Bandit and "Outlaw," another of his hot rods, were at the height of their fame, Revell, the plastic model kit maker, turned out so many kits that Ed was getting a *monthly* check for $3,000, based on just one cent for every kit sold.

Ed's favorite car stories are actually about people. A buddy named Doug came over dressed in a tuxedo, to help him pour plaster for Beatnik Bandit. Doug had been married several times and the tuxedo was his suit for special occasions. Doug's class act of doing the dirtiest work in his tuxedo touched Ed's sense of the ridiculous and from then on, Doug was "Dirty Doug."

Dick Cook was Ed's hammer mechanic. He taught Ed that a big hammer fixes most things. Ed was impressed one day when Cook was beating on an engine with his special hammer and it bounced

"Outlaw" is Ed's most famous T Bucket hot rod, powered by a Cadillac V–8.

off so hard that it hit him in the head and knocked him out. Since that time, this special technique is one that Ed claims he has not used, is not likely to use and does not recommend to people building rods!

Ed's approach to design is not the only thing that is unique. So is his construction technique. "Never draw a picture of a car before you build it. Anything looks good if an artist draws it," he has said. But then, Ed is a sculptor, not a car designer. He conceives and then executes by simply building and shaping as he goes. He occasionally builds models, but only as sculptures. He truly is a genius of design. Ed still owns the "Druid Princess," a vehicle he built for the "Addams Family" TV show. It was never used, however, as the show was cancelled just as he was finishing the project.

Over the years, Ed not only proved himself as a builder, but also as a drag racer. George "Bushmaster" Schreiber and Ed built and raced "Yellow Fang" from 1970 until 1975. Yellow Fang was one of America's best-known Top Fuel dragsters, pulling an ET of 7.80 seconds for a speed of 207 mph. After several years of promoting Yellow Fang in the United States and overseas, Ed had tired of drag racing, pulled the engine out of Yellow Fang and built one heck of a trike for tooling around the desert with Dirty Doug.

Ed's life as a wild man of California hot rodding was rudely interrupted in 1970. Nearly his entire life's work—hot rods and trikes—was stolen. His studio was literally swept clean of everything, including his savage guard dogs. Nothing was ever recovered, not his steam car project, his molds or his screens. At the time, Ed had a full-time staff of thirteen. The burglary so devastated him that he just walked away from it all. It still hurts him to talk about the robbery but Big Daddy came back, fourteen years later, stronger and very mellow.

He started yet another revolution in the hot rod industry. He built two wild trikes, including one with a glass replica of a chopped and channeled 1935 Ford coupe body tailored to fit the trike configuration. He returned to the imaginative approach that led to all those wild cars of twenty years ago.

Ed is an expert in V–8–powered trikes, and one of the many books he has published is a trike builder manual. His current trike is a V–6 Buick-powered monster called "Asphalt Angel."

During his absence, no one stepped into his position in the T-shirt business nor the hot rod and show car business, so he welcomed hot rodding back into his life. Big Daddy still has that high-energy drive to create and produce. He not only does the artwork, printing and publishing of a series of "How-To" books, but silk-screens all his T-shirts and caps.

He is back to building hot rods and trying out new ideas. In 1987 he sold Asphalt Angel and started on "Globe Hopper," a three-wheeled VW-powered

"Rat Fink," born on a table napkin and made famous on T-shirts across the world, was Ed's most successful and creative marketing project.

Ed hams it up for the camera. Dean Moon

152

1934 Ford. He drove this rod to Alaska as a side trip on his way to the Street Rod Nationals in 1988. Ed was refused entry to this event because some NSRA members said Globe Hopper was "not a true rod." Surprisingly, Ed had just attended the Canadian Street Rod Nationals, where he had been given a hero's welcome. Ed went back to the drawing board and began work on a four-wheeled, semi-monocoque Acura two-cam-powered roadster using Top Fuel dragster wheels up front.

He recently signed an agreement with Mattel, the toy maker, to produce a new line of Rat Fink toys and another deal to market Rat Fink shirts, towels, surfboards and logos. Revell has also re-released Ed's most popular plastic model kits.

With all this new activity, Ed recently left California with his wife Bev to live in Manti, Utah, because life was moving too fast and the air was too dirty. In the clear mountain air south of Salt Lake City, Ed works on Rat Fink projects and runs his mail order and design businesses. Soon, he'll be back on the road, trying out new ideas and with yet another perfect piece of cutting-edge hot rod technology.

Ed in his shop.

153

Chapter 26

Bill Stroppe

While some people feel that "a man can be measured by his worth," it's best to measure men like Bill Stroppe by their actions and accomplishments. Bill was never one to seek all the glory and riches for the work he did on behalf of countless racers and both professional and shoestring race efforts. It was enough for him to realize that he and the crew had done their best, and they were often rewarded with victories as well.

Rather than measuring Bill Stroppe's career by the riches he earned, it's more valid to measure it by all that he contributed to motorsports.

Bill's father ran a dairy and barbershop, but Bill had little interest in cows or cutting hair. His natural talents leaned toward mechanical fields and he was soon the official family mechanic. The fifteen-cow "Golden Jersey Dairy" catered to local customers, and it was Bill's job to deliver the milk in one of the two company Model T trucks.

At age twelve, getting the job done was a priority and Bill was the fastest delivery driver around. One of his customers, Floyd Henderson, ran a junkyard just down the street, where inquisitive young Stroppe discovered the innermost workings of the automobile.

By the age of fourteen, with the help of his father, Bill was running his own repair garage and gas station as his summer job. A 1932 Ford roadster came into Bill's hands and became his first race car. Testing was usually done on the streets of Long Beach or some of the old tracks around Los Angeles.

Bill took all of the auto shop courses at Long Beach Polytechnic High School taught by his new mentor, Floyd Nelson, who noticed Bill's mechanical talents and invited him to become part of the team that raced the "Multi-Ray Neon" Midget racer on the dirt tracks around Los Angeles.

In the summer of 1938, Bill was on the Multi-Ray Neon team which went to Denver to try its hand on the local dirt tracks. To relieve his chronic shortage of money, Bill tried the "Slide for Life." It called upon all of his youthful talents and courage to ride down the track on the back of the Midget, drop his back onto the track while holding onto a rope and slide on down the track. For a while, it worked fine.

His career as a stuntman, however, came to an abrupt end in California, when he discovered that the track surface was not conducive to sliding. On his last attempt, Bill did several flips, one of which completely ripped the seat out of his pants. The crowd loved it, but Bill decided that show business was not where he wanted to be.

During his last year in high school, Bill met another budding racer, Clay Smith. They both loved the dry lakes, the dirt tracks and boat racing. For the lakes, Bill built a Model T-powered racer that used a strange combination of a Chevy chassis, Model A rear end and Model T body. He was also running the Speedway circuit in his 1935 modified Ford roadster.

Smith also raced boats, which encouraged Bill to buy what appeared to be a revolutionary racing boat. He installed a new Ford flathead V–8 and went to the Long Beach boat races. His boat flew like a scalded cat up the main straight, but in the first 180 degree turn it flipped and sank like a 600–pound rock. Bill and his crew were forced to wait for the races to finish before they could recover their sunken speedster.

Bill accepted a job with Art Hall, a local Nash dealer who, a short time later, changed his franchise to a Lincoln-Mercury dealership, which later became Bill's key connection to the Ford Motor Company. He also took care of Hall's boating interests—which meant that boat racing was part of his regular racing week. He was also racing a midget and did well with it at the Terminal Island track.

With World War II looming, Bill joined the Naval Air Reserve at Long Beach in 1940. By late–1941, he was a full-time Navy man. The base commander, Earl DeLong, took Bill under his wing as his driver when he noticed his remarkable mechanical talents. It was also during this time that Bill married his sweetheart, Helen Tavasti.

The war took DeLong and Bill to sea aboard the "USS Casco." It proved to be a great partnership. Bill's unit received a Presidential Unit Citation for developing faster and safer methods of refueling seaplanes. His last call to action was during a tropical storm, refueling a large flying boat. While steadying the floundering vehicle, he was crushed and he dropped, badly injured, into the sea. The crew managed to haul him aboard and he was transferred to a hospital ship, where his recovery was slow and painful. Bill was back on board the Casco six weeks later, still not fully recovered, when Japan surrendered.

It was time to get back to the fast cars he loved the most, to the hot, dusty days at the dry lakes, the wild rides on the speedway and wet and furious boat racing. It didn't take long for Bill to get back in the fast lane.

Smith and Bill resumed their partnership in speed, with Bill purchasing a failed Kurtis Kraft Midget that he promptly turned into a winner. Johnny Mantz and Troy Ruttman drove for Bill, while Smith built the engines.

Bill also returned to boat racing. He was sponsored by Hall and built a new raceboat he called "Miss Art Hall." It was made out of plywood and powered with a Clay Smith-built Ford flathead six. The engine was not a typical racing motor. It had a

Bill Stroppe after winning the Mobilgas Economy Run in a Mercury sedan with Clay Smith as his partner in 1950.

155

handful of flaws that even Ford could not fix but which Smith soon had corrected with a little hot rod ingenuity. A few crank modifications and a new cam soon had Miss Art Hall tearing the Class 225 apart.

With Hall's financial help, the crew headed for Detroit to run in the Henry Ford Memorial Regatta. The "boys from California" soon showed their style, with Bill performing what could be called "water slaughter." Miss Art Hall out-performed everything else in the class.

Her performance caught the attention of Ford engineers, who wanted a closer look at what these "dang hot rodders" had done with the engine. Smith wanted to keep his engine's secrets, but he could see that a little cooperation might pay handsome dividends. His simple but effective hot rodder's knowledge left the engineers dumbfounded but appreciative, and they quickly changed Ford's production engine with a revised crank and a new cam.

From this adventure came the close association of Art Hall and Benson Ford, Sr., which soon reaped benefits for Bill, Smith and Hall. Smith's knack for promotion united him with Lincoln-Mercury and Bill, in the 1950 Mobilgas Economy Run. He made sure that the engine was "perfectly stock" while Bill checked out every mile of the 750 mile course. With the Mercury back together, they headed east to Kingman, Arizona, to do some extensive testing.

The testing and pre-running proved to be perfect preparation. Using every trick they knew, they drove the Mercury through hell and high water to outright victory—much to the surprise of the organizers and Benson Ford—achieving an amazing twenty-six miles to the gallon.

In 1951, Bill returned to the Mobilgas Economy Run and won the Outright Sweepstakes. The Economy Run became an annual event for him for the next ten years, though he never won the Outright cap again.

He purchased the first Kurtis Kraft 550S sports car for road racing and with this wild, toothy-looking, two-seater built by Frank Kurtis he soon had the competition tingling. Powered by a Smith-built Mercury flathead, Bill slid and blasted his way to a 1952 Sports Car Club of America road racing championship. He had found his niche, going fast in anything.

Bill and Smith formed a business partnership under the banner of "Stroppe and Smith" to campaign the special Mercury projects that now came under their wing. They were offered the chance to run in the great Mexican event, the Carrera Pan-American Road Race, under the sponsorship of Bob Estes, a Lincoln/Mercury dealer. Bill and Smith entered as a team for the next few years, leaving a mark on the stock car class like none before or since.

In 1951, Bill prepared and organized a Lincoln/Mercury for Smith and Troy Ruttman, but in 1952, Bill took the wheel again, along with Indy driver Johnny Mantz. The race was one of the most dangerous and bloody open-road races ever run, but the Stroppe/Mantz team placed second.

Bill's work was not confined to racing. He also fully prepared the three-car team and set up special roadside service facilities that made simple service work a breeze in the Mexican jungle. The fantastic success of the Mercurys in Mexico was directly related to Bill and Smith and their natural inclination to "do it right and do it fast." 1954 was another

Chief Petty Officer Stroppe in his Navy uniform.

Bill with his fenderless 1937 Ford coupe.

Tim Flock drove Bill Stroppe's Mercury convertible to a
win on the beach at Daytona in 1957.

The "Mermaid," a custom-bodied Mercury convertible
with a Stroppe-built motor, was driven to a record speed
of 159.9 mph at Daytona in 1957. This record gave Bill a
double-header at Daytona that year.

winning year in Mexico, and Bill's team was invited to appear on the "Ed Sullivan Show."

But 1955 was not such a good year. His friend and partner Clay Smith was killed at a track in DuQuion, Illinois, when a car spun off the track and rolled through the pits. It was a personal tragedy for Bill and a considerable blow to the business. Today, there is still a slight pause in Bill's voice when conversation turns to talk of Smith.

Also, the great Mexican road races ended in 1955. Bill had already formed a team and tested the vehicles, but with no place to race, the Lincoln/Mercury Division looked to other events to demonstrate its products' performance. Bill was quick to get Lincoln/Mercury interested in stock cars and the Daytona Speed Week.

For the 1956 Speed Week, Bill pulled a classic hot rodder's trick: "What you see is not what you get." Overnight, he built a trick, fuel-injected engine to run in a stock-bodied sedan in the Factory Experimental Class. The Mercury roared down the sand at 152 mph. Mercury loved the press, and Bill had work underway for another attempt in 1957. With Tim Flock at the wheel, the Mercury brought home the winning flag for Bill in the last convertible ever raced in stock cars. Art Chrisman drove the other Factory

Experimental Mercury convertible, which featured a streamlined nose and vertical stabilizer. He recorded a speed of 159 mph.

Bill moved on to NASCAR. His reputation for reliable and fast Fords kept him in steady work. He hired the best drivers, including Jimmy Bryan, Johnny Mantz, Sam Hanks, Troy Ruttman and Billy Meyers.

The withdrawal of Ford from direct motorsports competition in the late-fifties had a great impact on Bill and his organization. With Ford out of racing, Bill looked to other ventures to keep the cash flowing. Both he and Fran Hernandez became advisors to Autolite Spark Plugs.

Bill maintained strong contacts with Ford and Mercury, and Benson Ford, head of the Mercury Division, told Bill, "I realize you're going to have to move into some other work for a while, but don't move too far!" Benson knew Henry Ford had something in the works again, and wanted Bill to be ready.

Bill did private race car preparation for a while and did some high-temperature evaluations for GMC Trucks.

It didn't take long for Henry Ford II to return to racing with a vengeance. He had tried to buy out Ferrari but Enzo Ferrari had, not too politely, told him "No." Henry Ford decided he would take Enzo on, and Bill suddenly found that Mercury was back into racing.

In 1964, Bill hired Parnelli Jones to drive his new Mercury Marauder, and Jones proceeded to tear apart the competition, with eight major wins and a Pikes Peak title.

Bill's plans were executed by his trusted crew. Danny Eames, Herb Thomas, Cecil Bowman and Vern Houle were all in there, doing their best for him. Under his direction, they built a team of Mercury Comets for the 1964 East African Safari. They did this with their usual thoroughness, but the extremely rough terrain slaughtered the Comets.

Meanwhile, one of Bill's former employees, John Holman, united Bill and stock car racer Ralph Moody to form a team called "Holman-Moody-Stroppe." Their intention was to run Fords in NASCAR and on the USAC circuits. The partnership was successful and included a trip to Le Mans to work on the Ford GT–40 Mk II racers for the twenty-four-hour race.

Bill's partnership with Holman and Moody ended when he was offered other Ford projects. These projects included a return to Pikes Peak with Bobby Unser, which netted Ford another win, and the Pantera project, which got under way in 1972 with Bill contracting to prepare all the Italian-built sports coupes for dealers.

Bill's greatest work was yet to come. The great off-road racing age was just around the corner, and he was headed for Mexico again via the Riverside Raceway. In 1965, Ford had introduced the Bronco

Parnelli Jones set a new stock car record in 1964 with this Stroppe-prepared Mercury Marauder on Pikes Peak.

Bill and Parnelli Jones in Baja, driving a Stroppe-prepared Bronco.

4 x 4. It was the perfect vehicle for off-road adventures. He entered the Riverside Grand Prix, an off-road event, for a lark. It was apparently "just what the doctor ordered." It didn't take long for him to see the potential of off-road racing, and he was in the line-up for the first Baja 1,000 in 1967.

Bill teamed up with Parnelli Jones and spent the next five years racing in the deserts of Nevada and the Baja Peninsula. The pair won numerous events, with Jones driving and Bill riding shotgun in Stroppe-built and -prepared racers. The most famous was "Big Oly," the Olympia Beer-sponsored, two-wheel-drive Bronco.

Bill's Ford-based team grew to fifteen vehicles in 1973 and with more and more off-road experience under his belt, Bill became a walking encyclopedia, able to look at problems from both the driver's and builder's side.

In the mid-seventies, Jones moved away from off-road racing and Bill stopped riding shotgun. Ford had other projects for him to deal with and other racers had cars for him to build. One Ford project involved chasing a balloon across the country as it zig-zagged its way from California to the East Coast via Mexico and Illinois.

Once when Bill and Jones were in Baja an old friend, Josefina Ramo, came to them with a request: The community around Rancho Santa Inez needed a

Bill does yet another TV interview on behalf of Ford and his team.

Bill Stroppe

medical clinic. Bill and Jones took the idea to heart and with the help of hundreds of friends and companies, they pushed and shoved the project to completion. Three years later, the tiny community of 300 had a fully-equipped facility, which is now part of the regular Flying Samaritans route. Bill had returned to Baja a little of what Baja had given to him.

He continued to build off-road racing trucks for some of the world's best drivers, not all Fords, however. Bill's shop built Hall's Dodge off-road racers and a series of Ramcharger race trucks for an event in Kenya.

His facility in Long Beach is not far from the dairy on Signal Hill where he began his journey into hot rod history. He continues to work closely with the Ford Motor Company, running its brake-testing vehicles under a special "City Cycle" program and maintaining its press fleet on the West Coast for magazine and newspaper folks.

Bill has many friends, ranging from CEOs to old school buddies with whom he still spends time. He is a quiet, unassuming man who, to outsiders, could be a bus driver or a local mechanic. But his friends all say the same thing, "Stroppe's the one guy you can count on to be there, rain or shine, a gentleman's hot rodder to the end."

Chapter 27

Bobby and Bill Summers

Think back to a time, oh, thirty or thirty-five years ago. Men like Ike and JFK were directing the United States, wrestling with the challenges of a still-maturing modern world. In the western United States, meanwhile, pockets of young men gathered in garages, on back roads, in the desert and on the salt flats to wrestle with what they considered the challenges ("need more horsepower," "need more style") of the golden age of hot rodding.

A couple of those "kids" were two brothers in Ontario, California, Bobby and Bill Summers. While they worked hard to make their cars look good and go fast, they could never have realized the seemingly indelible mark they would one day make on the world of speed. Their first hot rods went fast by their early standards, but they would be considered mere chase cars compared to the high-powered rockets they would one day create and pilot to fame.

They kicked around with all sorts of hot cars at first, then finally settled on building race cars for the Bonneville Speed Week. Their first attempts were rather "soft, performance-wise," as Billy put it, but they were learning. After several attempts, success came with a 1929 Model A roadster, which ran 175 mph on gasoline.

This was the turning point for the brothers. The speed bug had bitten them, and they built a series of race cars that brought home a record every year.

Bill (left) and Bob posed with the Goldenrod at Bonneville. By today's standards, the almost complete absence of sponsor stickers or logos is staggering. The Summers Brothers' logo appears on the sides and the nose of the machine, but there are virtually no other markings on the shell. In sketches in a publicity kit issued after the record-setting run, sponsor stickers were shown on various components beneath the shell.

Bill (right) consulted with George Hurst about work on the Goldenrod at Bonneville. The car used four Chrysler Hemis that were almost stock except they had fuel injection and exhaust headers.

The team's crew prepared the Goldenrod for another run at the Salt Flats. The speed machine used two engines to power the front wheels and another pair of engines to power the rears, and each wheel had independent suspension.

Eventually, the project developed into building a streamliner (the equivalent of building an F-1 car). This car was known as the "Pollywog," a front-engine beast that ran an impressive 323 mph, much to everyone's surprise.

After cracking the magical 300-mph barrier, the brothers set their sights on the world's Land Speed Record; after all, they were in the low-300s and the record was just a lick over 400. Another 80 mph is not that big a jump, they figured.

Donald Campbell held the record at the time with "Bluebird" at 403 mph. The brothers were buoyed by their earlier success and decided to build a challenger to his car.

They spent hundreds of hours at the drawing board and came up with a car they hoped could bring back the record to America. They were confident that they could do this, as they had the driving skills and the technical knowledge necessary. Their biggest stumbling block was the lack of money needed for such an ambitious project, so they went in search of sponsors.

Firestone liked the idea and offered to produce a special tire, rated in excess of 400 mph. Mobil Oil had a record of sponsoring such attempts and made a sizeable contribution. George Hurst of the Hurst/Campbell Company supplied money and technical support and Chrysler donated four new 426 Hemis. The boys were on their way.

They ran a series of proposed body shapes through extensive wind tunnel testing at Cal Tech University. From this research, they concluded that the best shape would be a narrow, long, cigar-like tube. "Goldenrod" was born.

To achieve this shape, they built a steel frame using two inch by six inch lower rails. The engines were mounted in-line and coupled in pairs, back to back. The front pair drove the front wheels and the rear pair drove the rear wheels. Power was transferred through a pair of special five-speed Spicer transmissions using Schiefer double-disc clutches. Surprisingly, it was designed with four-wheel, independent suspension. It was just a whisker over 10 meters long and 1.3 meters wide. The car was then skinned with a hand-formed 3003 aluminum body. The important stopping systems used disc brakes on the drivetrain and a pair of Deist parachutes for braking after the speed had dropped to below 250 mph.

They had very specific design criteria, and construction started on January 1, 1965. The racer was ready for its first attempt in September that same year. Bobby was the driver, and on his first pass down the Bonneville Land Speed Record Course, he ran 250 mph. In three subsequent runs, he raised that to 390 mph, still using regular gasoline, but before they could manage to crack the 400–mph barrier, it rained on the course, closing it down for several weeks.

They returned months later with a few modifications to try again, but one of the Hemis bit the bullet, destroying itself internally. Their record attempt was again canned. At this time, there was intense competition to be the fastest man on four wheels, and the course was solidly booked for weeks. Their next chance came when Art Arfons, who was attempting to challenge the Land Speed Record for jet-powered cars, cancelled his week's booking.

They returned to Bonneville and on November 12, 1965, got Goldenrod revved up. The car flew down and then back up the course for a two-way average of 409.695 mph; a new Land Speed Record! This figure still stands—twenty-one years later. An interesting point about Goldenrod is that, although it was a high-tech race car in 1965, it was powered by Chrysler engines that were factory-stock except for fuel injection and exhaust headers. Each Hemi was rated for a peak of only 700 hp.

Goldenrod is still in the hands of the Summers brothers and has just returned to California after nine tours in Europe. Interestingly, the brothers received

Bill Summers

Bob Summers

In 1959, the brothers ran this Class B Modified roadster
with a 300-ci Chrysler to a speed of 240.38 mph on the salt.

UNITED STATES AUTO CLUB   CLASS   <u>UNLIMITED</u>
FEDERATION INTERNATIONALE de L'AUTOMOBILE   SPEED TRIALS

              <u>BONNEVILLE SALT BEDS - UTAH - USA</u>
Date   <u>NOVEMBER 12, 1965</u>
USAC Sanction No. <u>65 SR 7</u>
F. I. A. Listing

<u>GOLDENROD</u>   <u>11 MILE STRAIGHTAWAY</u>   <u>BOBBY SUMMERS</u>
Automobile   Course   Driver

<u>FLYING 1 KILO</u>
Distance

North Run	10:17AM	Recording	Time	Speed M. P. H.
Finish Time		3:47:02.131		
Start Time		3:46:56.678	5.453	410.220
South Run	09:25AM			
Finish Time		2:55:31.887		
Start Time		2:55:26.421	5.466	409.245
Time - - Two Directions			5.460	
Official Average	<u>409.695</u>			

We, the undersigned, served as the regularly appointed officials of the Contest Committee
of the United States Auto Club and Federation Internationale de L'Automobile, in
connection with the above times and record run of   <u>BOBBY SUMMERS</u>
                            driving the
        <u>GOLDENROD</u>
under United States Auto Club Sanction
, and we HEREBY CERTIFY that the above times and speeds are correct as shown and

The official report from the FIA and USAC shows that
Bob made runs at speeds of 410.220 mph and 409.245 mph
for a record average speed of 409.695 mph.

This single-engine streamliner preceded the Goldenrod by several years and was a good learning tool for Bob and Bill.

no financial rewards for their efforts, apart from the money to build and run the car. They only received a "Certificate of Performance." Bill Summers recalls, "You know, all we were thinking about at the time was just getting the record. All we wanted was the recognition. A recognition for our technology."

With the Land Speed Record in the bag, they had the incentive and found financial backing to

In this Hemi-powered Plymouth, Bob set a series of long-distance records at Bonneville after setting his world record.

Bill Summers ran 174 mph in this streamliner, the Jaz Products Special, in 1989.

start "Summers Brothers Inc." They were the first manufacturers specializing in drivetrain components for high-performance applications. Suddenly, they were "the ones who knew" and speed freaks of all types and sizes beat a path to their door. From a small one-shop operation, Summer Brothers Inc. has grown into a five-shop business that manufactures the very best in driveline products. Their products are race-quality components built to exceed by five, ten or twenty times the breaking point of the original product they replace.

Summers Brothers products include aluminum radiators, axles, axle housings, spools, bearing caps and gear drives. Bill Summers has described the axles as "unmatched in strength. Doubling the diameter of an axle from one inch to two inches increases the torsional strength eight times." While it is not their practice to work on the theory of "double everything and hope that it works," it is easy to see

that the thicker you can build your axles and the heavier you can spline them, the stronger they will be.

The company continues to develop its world-renowned expertise in drivetrain strength and horsepower management. It has been "the common-sense approach to technology" that has put them at the forefront of the high-performance industry. Like other leading high-performance manufacturers, they have always followed the policy, "Quality is Number One."

Bill has moved on to other projects and Bob runs Summers Brothers Inc. Bill's work allows him time to return each year to the Bonneville Salt Flats to run his own streamliner. He loves the salt like a sailor loves the sea and he's still looking for the edge that will keep the Summers' name planted firmly in the record books.

Chapter 28

Mickey Thompson

Mickey Thompson might have become the greatest race car driver of all time if he hadn't been such a successful businessman. Already a successful racer by 1960, he came up with winners as an aftermarket equipment manufacturer and a race promoter, and he wisely committed his time to running his businesses. Even though he didn't race as long as some other veterans, he still made his mark as a winner on several types of tracks, and then went on to develop some of the finest, richest and most popular race organizations in history.

He was born in 1929 to an Irish family and christened Marion Lee Thompson. Mickey grew up in El Monte, California, where his father was a policeman. A bright student in school, Mickey did not always accept the standard ways of education, especially if he could find a shorter way to an answer.

Even as a youngster, Mickey showed strong mechanical skills, but he disdained formal procedures or techniques. In school, the only subjects that interested him were math, shop classes and athletics. Everything else was "a complete bore." He had no patience with unnecessarily tedious procedures when there was a more efficient way to reach the same goal.

His early teenage years were tough. Being a policeman, his father didn't tolerate Mickey's interest and involvement in hot rodding, and it was Mickey's desire to be a hot rodder. In time, his environment, skills and interest developed his talent as a driver, an advanced fabricator and promoter of the hot rod image and lifestyle.

He had little money to buy the scarce performance parts available, so he built his own. He made boxed rods and fabricated a quick-change rear end from a 1936 Ford center section and a couple of sections of scrap tube. He also built a twin flathead-powered 1932 Bantam coupe for the dry lakes.

His unblown coupe would never go over 194 mph at Bonneville, so in 1953, he installed a Chrysler Hemi with a 4–71 GMC supercharger. This innovation was one of his many firsts in the automotive performance field.

Mickey lived for fast cars, using his aggressive and ambitious nature to build better ways to go

Marion Lee "Mickey" Thompson: racer, businessman, entrepreneur and promoter.

Mickey and Danny Ongais (right) after their successful endurance trials on the Bonneville Salt Flats in a pair of Ford Mustangs.

racing. His ideas and work changed more than one form of motorsports forever. In the mid-fifties, he pioneered the slingshot dragster with the cockpit behind the rear axle to increase the traction at the rear wheels. In a dragster of this style, he was the first to drive through the quarter-mile at over 150 mph.

It was not only drag racing that attracted Mickey. From 1955 until 1957, he drove a Cadillac-Kurtis in West Coast sports car events, never doing particularly well but always having fun.

In 1960, he became the first American to drive over 400 mph, when he pushed his four-wheel-drive Challenger, equipped with four Pontiac engines, to 406.6 mph one way at Bonneville. At the time, it was the fastest anyone had ever driven a true automobile. Unfortunately, he broke a driveshaft during the return run, so he was not able to get the two-way average he needed for a world's Land Speed Record.

In 1960 and 1961, he used two streamlined dragsters, "Assault" and "Attempt," and a half-dozen modified Pontiac engines ranging from 90 to 503 ci to

set new standing-start acceleration figures for the kilometer and the mile in six classes.

Other forms of motorsports were attracting his attention. In 1961, the Indianapolis 500 became his dream and the next year, he entered the first stock block, mid-engine car ever to qualify. It used an aluminum Buick V–8 in a chassis built by a former Lotus engineer. Mickey hired Dan Gurney to drive the race. He didn't win, but the car went down in history as the first modern mid-engine Indy car.

(That same year, Jack Chrisman drove a Thompson-built, aluminum Pontiac-powered AA/Top Fuel dragster to the NHRA Championship, defeating Don Garlits in the finals at the Nationals.)

Mickey's achievements in 1962 won him the annual D. A. Mechanic's Awards for both Indy car and drag racing. It was the only time that the prestigious crew chief's honor went to one man in two different categories.

During this same period, Mickey also did some racing of his own. From 1960 until 1963, he raced powerboats, running in twenty-seven consecutive events without winning. One accident left him with two crushed vertebrae and paralyzed legs. He was told it might be months before he would walk again, but with his characteristic determination, he was on his feet in two weeks.

One reason that Mickey may not have done better in sports cars or powerboat racing is that they didn't offer the latitude for innovation he'd exploited in drag racing and at Bonneville and Indianapolis. His success was bound up in his ability to out-think the opposition and use a new idea that hadn't been tried before. Mickey figured that if all you did was

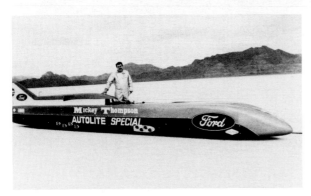

Mickey with his record-setting Ford Autolite Special on the salt at Bonneville.

Mickey and his assistant Pat Foster work on one of Mickey's four-engined, Ford-powered land speed cars.

imitate the most successful combination, you could only hope to equal its performance. He had to go further; he had to start at the point of departure.

Inevitably, Thompson the innovator became Mickey Thompson the entrepreneur, establishing the "Mickey Thompson Equipment Company" in 1959. At the outset, he concentrated on high-performance items for Pontiac engines, as they were engines he had used for most of his own racing efforts. In 1962, he entered ten Pontiac-powered cars, which won in ten classes in various races, much to his and Pontiac's delight.

In time, the "M/T" logo appeared on a broad range of equipment for several makes. In 1964, he formed another company, "Mickey Thompson Tires," to market a full line of tires and wheels for high-performance cars.

As if all that wasn't enough, Mickey was also active in promoting races and shows. From 1955 until 1964, he managed the famed Lions Drag Strip in Long Beach, California. There, he dug the postholes by hand, bought scrap pipe for the fence posts, built the timing tower and sold pit passes. Some 10,000 people showed up for opening day.

From 1961 until 1964, he staged auto and boat shows in Los Angeles. By the late-sixties, it might seem that Mickey Thompson had seen and done it all, from the dragstrip to the dry lakes to the speedway.

But this was just the dawning of the age of Mickey Thompson. In the late-sixties, he began building the first monocoque Funny Car, a Ford Mustang Mach 1 powered by a Ford Boss 429 engine. By the end of 1970, Mickey had run two Mach 1's, a Ford Maverick and the monocoque Mustang Funny Car using drivers Danny Ongais and Mike Van Sant. Both drivers rarely lost a race.

But at about that time, a whole new form of motorsport called off-road racing had emerged, giving Thompson yet another challenge as a car builder, driver and promoter. Ford bowed out of motorsports and Mickey was ready for a change.

The National Off-Road Racing Association (NORRA) had begun organizing regular cross-country races in the wastelands of Mexico's Baja and California peninsula, while the Mint Hotel in Las Vegas was running similar events in the deserts of southern Nevada.

"Challenger I," the speed machine that just missed setting a new world Land Speed Record at Bonneville. R. Metz

Mickey was fascinated by the off-road sport. Soon, when he wasn't driving a pickup truck or dune buggy in the NORRA or Mint events, he was flying his own plane over them to observe the action. He was convinced that off-road racing could be developed into a terrific spectator sport within the confines of a closed course, just like sports car racing.

The idea wasn't completely new. There had been attempts at spectator-oriented off-road competition during the sixties, and NORRA had staged such an event at Riverside International Raceway in 1971.

In 1973, Mickey formed "Short Course Off-Road Enterprises" (SCORE) and presented the first

Mickey at work on yet another of his four-engined Bonneville cars. Dean Moon

SCORE Off-Road Championships at Riverside. With NORRA's emphasis on long-distance events and SCORE's focus on the short course, the two organizations seemed complementary rather than competitive.

Following a successful NORRA event in Baja in mid–1973, the Baja, California, city government revoked the association's permission to stage races south of the border and a Mexican group took over. It held its first event later that year. Unfortunately, the directors of the new group lacked the experience to stage a successful long-distance contest and were unable to pay the winning drivers.

Several weeks later, the winners began receiving their checks and, according to rumors never confirmed nor denied, Mickey had contributed the funds to pay them. The Mexican group was dissolved and SCORE was given a contract by the Baja government to organize long-distance races in the region. In one swoop, SCORE had displaced NORRA as the major organizer of cross-country off-road events.

Still a competitor at heart, Mickey withdrew from the day-to-day operation of SCORE because he wanted to be free to take part in its races, which he did on a regular basis. He drove high-powered, V–8–equipped buggies of his own design. They were blindingly fast, but with his hard-charging driving style, they usually broke. His off-road racing was becoming a replay of his unsuccessful efforts years before in sports cars and powerboat racing.

Finally, in the 1982 Baja 1,000, he gained his long-sought, off-road victory. Ironically, though, it was in a borrowed VW-powered Raceco buggy. Mickey and Terry Smith co-drove the 900–mile race, emerging as overall winners against all comers in all classes.

That was Mickey's last serious effort at driving competitively. He had promised his wife Trudy that he would hang up his helmet if he won in Baja, and he kept his word.

Mickey's enthusiasm for off-road racing as a spectator sport had grown. In 1978, with Trudy's help, he started another organization, "Mickey Thompson Entertainment Group" (MTEG) to stage short-course, off-road races. This time, the races were run in stadiums where all the action would be within the view of the entire audience.

Mickey Thompson's Off-Road Championship Gran Prix, as the MTEG racing series was called, began at the Los Angeles County Fairgrounds and soon appeared at other southern California facilities, including the Los Angeles Coliseum, Pasadena Rose Bowl, Anaheim Stadium and Jack Murphy Stadium

Mickey—dirty, tired and exhausted—after winning the Buggy Class in the Baja 1,000.

in San Diego. It also spread across the country to Houston, Indianapolis and Pontiac, Michigan.

During the mid-eighties, MTEG became Mickey and Trudy's primary occupation. By 1987, he had sold his interest in several of his earlier enterprises, including SCORE, to concentrate on promoting the stadium races. Mickey began to delegate increasing responsibility to the MTEG staff so that he could spend more time with his wife and virtually retire from the management side of his company.

It was not to be. In mid-March of 1988, Mickey and Trudy were shot and killed in the driveway of their home as they prepared to leave for the MTEG offices.

Suddenly, the "Mickey T" era in motorsports history had come to a horrible end. Hundreds of racers, spectators and friends attended the double funeral.

With Mickey and Trudy's deaths, a bit of every racing enthusiast died, too. The entire gambit of motorsports had been touched by Mickey. Mickey left behind a great following who will always remember him as a champion in his own right, especially when the term "innovation" is used.

Chapter 29

Linda Vaughn

For some beauty queens, the high times end as soon as the tiara is passed on to a successor. For Linda Vaughn, however, success and the sense of being a winner were not restricted to the time constraints of any "reign" beneath a bejeweled crown. No, she was a success from the start, and remained one throughout her career in the automotive world.

Linda poses with a Hurst shifter and a Corvette for a magazine ad.

A beauty queen or poster girl for a shifter company would hardly seem like an obvious role model for young women, but that's exactly what Linda Vaughn was during the sixties and seventies. She never let herself play the role of "just a beauty queen" whose value was only skin deep, and she never diminished or hid her obvious physical beauty because she felt she was being exploited.

Instead, she used both her mind and her beauty in a combination that made her a successful businesswoman and an incredibly popular representative of the automotive industry.

If she had a failing, it's that she stole attention away from the beautiful, fast cars and the great drivers; because of crowd response at car shows and races, it just worked out that way.

Linda comes from a family background that includes German, Irish and Cree Indian ancestors. She was one of thirteen children in her family, and she was always one of the curious, "how does this work?" ones. Her family was torn apart when her parents divorced, but she remained with her mother, Mae, and acquired the strength that made her so successful in an industry and an era dominated by men.

At age sixteen, Linda graduated from Dalton, Georgia, high school, and she was already certified as a dental technician. She had loftier aspirations, though, and began to pursue them when she won the title of Miss Dalton 1961. When she went to the Georgia State Fair to compete for the Miss Georgia Poultry crown, she had to lie about her age and claim she was eighteen. "I was kind of 'developed' for a sixteen-year-old and could pass for eighteen," she recalled. She stood out in the field of 200 contestants and won the title.

One of her next victories came in the Miss Atlanta International Raceway contest, which she entered and won when she turned eighteen for real. Part of her job was to help the speedway promote its big annual NASCAR event, so she and race star "Fireball" Roberts did the Twist on the track as a public relations stunt.

The goal was to generate publicity, and it worked. Linda became an overnight celebrity as photos and film footage of her and Roberts appeared in newspapers, magazines and television from coast-to-coast.

She had also become Miss Atlanta, which was so time-consuming that she had to quit her job as a dental assistant, a position she had held since finishing high school.

Linda collected another crown as "Queen of Speed," beating all local beauty queens from the South's major stock car tracks. Her popularity soon had her up front at the best events, including riding in the pace car at the 1962 Daytona 500. During this time, she became familiar with and among many of the faces and places of the early NASCAR circuit, and she used her looks and personality to attract and entertain the crowds.

The men in the public relations department at Pure Oil Company soon recognized her talent and at Roberts' suggestion, hired her as "Miss Firebird" to ride on the company's famous "Firebird Float."

This pre-race procession landed Linda a Miss Firebird photo spread in *Esquire* magazine in 1963. The Miss Firebird deal lasted only three years, though, because the company was absorbed by Union Oil and the promotional program was disbanded.

Hurst Performance had used the same beauty queen promotional idea with great success. Under the banner of "Miss Golden Shifter," several young women had appeared on Hurst's behalf at races and shows. Jenene Walsh and Pat Flannery had toured with Hurst as Miss Golden Shifter girls, but in 1966, the company decided to put a new twist on its publicity program.

In cooperation with *Hot Rod* magazine, Hurst ran a competition to find a new Miss Golden Shifter girl. Linda figured she had a good chance of landing the job, so she flew to California and met with Ray Brock, publisher of *Hot Rod,* and interviewed with George Hurst. She knew the competition would be tough.

On the night of the final judging, Linda's personality and developing business insight helped her win the title, along with a fully-equipped GTO. She made a dynamic presentation on what she could do for Hurst to the board of directors, and she won.

The previous winners had each held the title for a year, but Linda held it continuously for thirteen years. She had a strong view of what she and Hurst could achieve together. She was not just another pretty face but was determined to be a major-league player in the promotional side of the company.

Linda (standing) and the other Hurstettes, rode in the "Miss Golden Shifter" Oldsmobile in a pre-race parade at the Indy 500.

Hurst Vice President Jack Duffy recalled those times: "I figured Linda would be another of George Hurst's 'girlfriends,' but as she told me straight up, 'I don't sleep with the boss, so let's get on [with] the project.'"

"I also had to teach them I was a team player with more than a passing interest in auto racing," Linda added.

In his capacity as director of the company's public relations program, Duffy became her close

This photo was used in a print ad for Hurst-Olds.

friend and advisor. Linda's winning ways also made her a close friend to Hurst and his family.

Her first day of work was at the 1966 Winternationals. It was the day that showed Hurst and Duffy how wise their decision had been; not only were they pleased, but she, too, was overwhelmed with her success that day. She finished it exhausted

and in love with the sport of drag racing and its people.

Her instant success brought with it a demanding schedule of appearances at hundreds of race tracks across the country. So, she assembled a group of twelve "similarly equipped," voluptuous blondes known as the "Hurstettes."

This left Linda available for major events, where she proved to be so popular that it would take her thirty minutes or longer to move between the press tent and the Hurst stand as she talked with the admiring crowd who wanted to meet her and get her autograph.

During the Vietnam War era, she toured military bases and hospitals for nearly five years with the Hurst Armed Forces Club. She visited Vietnam several times. She would walk up to the microphone and tell the troops that she didn't dance or sing but was there to talk to them. She would conclude with, "I was hired to do publicity for the company, so I am trying to do it the best way I know." The troops went wild, whooping it up every time Linda walked on stage. She loved it and so did they.

Her Hurst Armed Forces Club appearances also took her to Puerto Rico, San Juan and dozens of military bases across the country. Requests for appearances by Linda came from hundreds of other events and organizations, ranging from Formula One races to charity telethons. Despite this hectic

This photo was used in ads for the Hurst "Shotgun" torque converter.

Linda (right) presided over the presentation of a Hurst-Olds to Tony Hulman (in car), long-time president of the Indianapolis Motor Speedway.

Linda's 1975 Miss Hurst publicity photo.

Linda was so well known at the peak of her career that
Hurst listed her name among the top products it featured
in this ad.

Linda Vaughn, 1990.

pace, Linda also managed to hit all the major trade events for Hurst and to do a series of ads for them.

She married Bill Tidwell on December 2, 1972, during Lions Drag Strip's "Last Drag Race," an event formally dedicated to the newlyweds. Many thought this would be the end of Linda Vaughn as Miss Golden Shifter, but her work with Hurst continued for another four years. She and Tidwell built a parts business but eventually divorced in the early-eighties.

Through those many years with Hurst, Linda had two people backing her up: "Doc" Watson and Duffy, who became an important part of her extended road family, helping her deal with every facet of her life and business.

In 1976, she decided to step aside as the Golden Shifter Girl to concentrate on radio and TV advertising, but she did a farewell ride with the huge shifter handle during the 1976 NHRA Nationals. The public, however, wouldn't let her stop, and many letters requesting her return hit the Hurst headquarters mailroom. She soon returned and attended as many events as before.

In 1989, she was still hard at work, making 134 appearances and traveling hundreds of thousands of miles, flying across the country from her home in southern California. Events such as the Daytona 500

176

and NHRA Winternationals became a second home.

Linda continued to wear an outrageous selection of outfits at these events. She would often appear in a golden fishnet bikini or a tight-fitting miniskirt made by her mother.

In recent years, with the Mr. Gasket Company taking over Hurst, Linda continued in her public relations role, appearing at a demanding array of events and shows.

"The difference with Linda is her magic combination of 'beauty plus brains'," according to many of her close friends. Like others in the performance industry, Linda knows many automotive people, but few can command the attention of Lee Iacocca and other CEO's the way she can.

Linda's good-natured style has opened the hearts of many, and her bubbling personality, broad smile and ability to recall names like a super-computer have not gone unrecognized by the industry or its leaders. Linda won a *Car Craft* magazine "Ollie Award" for her contributions to drag racing, and in 1987, the Specialty Equipment Manufacturers Association (SEMA) made her "Person of the Year." She was also inducted into the SEMA "Hall of Fame."

Top-rated racing pros in every arena of auto racing know her as a friend, not just as Miss Golden Shifter Girl. She counts Parnelli Jones, Don Garlits, Kenny Bernstein, A. J. Foyt, "Grumpy" Jenkins, Emmo Fittipaldi and Mario Andretti as part of her extended family of friends. The same can be said for her group of music and film associates, who include Bruce Springsteen, Neil Diamond, Gene Hackman and Paul Newman.

Linda is also a movie actress. She appeared in the movie "Cannonball Run" with Burt Reynolds, playing Linda Vaughn, the Queen of Speed.

When folks talk about auto racing and drivers, some of the names might not ring a bell. But everyone knows the name "Linda," or "Miss Golden Shifter."

Madison Avenue could not have invented a public relations concept as effective as Linda. She is a natural and knows the game, the players, her fans and the industry she represents. Her celebrity status is recognized throughout the performance and motorsports industries. At drag races, NASCAR events and the trade show circuit, Linda is still a major attraction representing Mr. Gasket and Hurst. Her schedule is still hectic, but signing autographs and shaking hands with her fans still puts a smile on her face, just like the day she first stepped into the pit lane at the 1966 Winternationals as Hurst's "Miss Golden Shifter."

Linda's life during the past few years has had its ups and downs, including a bout with cancer and a broken heart. But she is back, working the crowd, laughing and smiling with the millions of fans who are all in love with the "great-looking blonde from Georgia."

Chapter 30

"Von Dutch" (Kenneth Howard)

Compared to a car builder like Craig Breedlove or a parts manufacturer like Vic Edelbrock, Kenneth "Von Dutch" Howard didn't contribute much *physi-* *cally* to the sport of hot rodding. He did, however, contribute greatly to its style and art, which is to say that he helped to dramatically shape and define the culture and image of the sport.

Born Kenneth Howard in 1924, Von Dutch grew up in Watts in the shadow of the famous Watts Towers. His father was the sign writer and graphics artist

Kenneth Howard, better known as "Von Dutch." Pat Ganahl

An example of Von Dutch pinstripes on the rear of a white 1934 Ford three-window coupe. His touch with striping turned it into an art.

for the Western Exterminator Company and designed its famous cartoon character, an exterminator with a hammer, looking at a mouse.

Von Dutch was a natural with his hands. He had an eye for the mechanical and as a teen, attended Frank Wiggins Trade School. He was apparently not such a fine student of the books but was rather good at technical drawing. He learned to play the flute and sketched his famed flying eyeball. He drew continuously and developed a taste for the finer talents of German engineers of the thirties. Through this, he became an expert on every type of motorcycle and its engineering.

At first, he worked in an engraving shop in Compton, but later moved to a motorcycle shop owned by his friend, George Birop. One day a sign writer was booked to stripe a motorcycle tank but never showed up; Von Dutch offered to stripe the tank the next day. He had never actually done any striping but when he picked up his father's sign writing brushes, he discovered his latent talent.

By this time, he had developed a love of German engineering and culture. His nickname of "Von Dutch" is a derivation of "von Deutschland," which means "from Germany."

The Korean conflict intervened and he spent a stint overseas in the Air Force. Military life did not agree with him and he was discharged after two years for "borrowing" a piano to use in his barracks. His time in the military didn't help his alcohol problem either, and following his discharge, he fought that battle for a number of years.

In 1954, Von Dutch was working at the Barris brothers' shop, Competitive Motors, in Hollywood. It was around this time that his talent for striping reached its zenith. He developed complex shapes which became standard pinstriping concepts for the next thirty years. For the next ten years, he worked around Los Angeles, striping cars, working as a gunsmith and having a good time.

The stories about Von Dutch pinstriping each side of a single vehicle differently are apparently true, according to Ed Roth. "If Dutch felt bored with striping it all over again on the other side, he would simply start on a new design."

"After all, you can see only one side at a time," Dutch said.

He married and moved to Arizona. The father of two daughters, married life did not suit him; neither did Arizona. He traveled to Australia and worked his way about the country, eventually returning to California. He continued to do odd pinstriping jobs, restored motorcycles and worked for

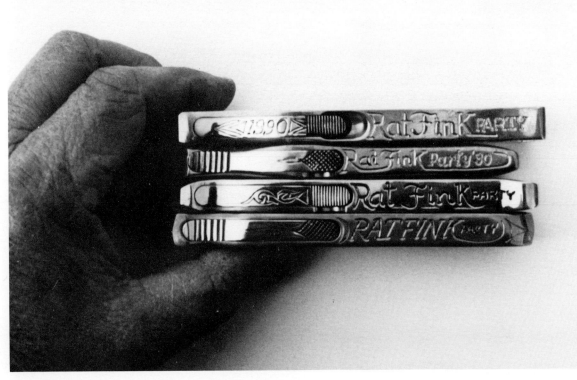

A set of Von Dutch knives made for Ed Roth's 1990 "Rat Fink Reunion." These were collectors' items the moment they were produced.

Jimmy Brucker's "Cars of the Stars" museum in Hollywood.

During this time, he also started building a few movie cars. Among them were a Bearcat Speedster-style vehicle and a miniature speedster powered by a Crosley four for the Steve McQueen movie "Reevers." He also worked on the movie, doing explosives work and producing artwork for movie sets.

When the car museum closed, Von Dutch moved to Santa Paula to oversee what remained of the Cars of the Stars collection belonging to Brucker.

He also resumed painting and drawing motorcycles and pursued his love of making knives. His knives have become sought-after items. Many times, he used scraps mixed with a variety of exotic woods,

ivory and metals for handles and scabbards. His knives are innovative and detailed with engraved surfaces, trick scabbards and custom-made, spring-loaded locking devices.

His other artwork is equally creative and done in the Von Dutch tradition. According to Ed Roth, Von Dutch believed that, "If it's been done, don't do it."

He has recently been building an ultra-light aircraft of his own design and is something of a recluse. He is still living hard and his recent artistic work has been some of the most creative and interesting in the field—just as in his early years of hot rodding. As usual, it has been done with an irreverent distaste for what's the "norm."

Some Von Dutch custom knives, including one (at bottom) made for the 1990 "Rat Fink Reunion."

Chapter 31

Ed Winfield

It's virtually impossible to determine the precise point at which hot rodding was born. It might be as easy to pick a Kentucky Derby winner from the sports section of a Japanese newspaper.

But the consensus is that the honor of the sport's true founder should rightfully be awarded to Ed Winfield. In fact, he's been called, "The Father of Hot Rodding."

The crowd of Ascot lined the fence in 1924 for a look at Ed, who had pulled up to pose for a cameraman. It's remarkable to think that racers competed with virtually no safety gear at the time. Instead of fireproof suits, which were still years away, racers like Ed wore white shirts, ties and waistcoats. His only safety gear to speak of were his goggles.

Born in 1901, Winfield was a car nut from his earliest days. He had a large collection of reading material on all mechanical subjects and by eight, was working part-time in a blacksmith shop.

He lived close to the Durand brothers, Sam and Harland. One Saturday afternoon with the senior Durands gone, the boys stripped the family Model T down to basics and spent the afternoon racing it around the field.

Ed enrolled in the local trade school section of the YMCA, blending his basic mechanical knowledge with first-hand hot rod and blacksmithing experience.

Automobiles took center stage for Ed, and he dodged about town trying to get behind the wheel of any automobile he could find. One afternoon, he borrowed a 1908 Maxwell and thrashed it about town. He found the steepest hill and ran the car flat out down the hill; 60 mph was as fast as the Maxwell would go. He found out later that his performance had not gone unnoticed; his father engaged him in a very pointed father-and-son talk which Ed never forgot.

As fate would have it, Ed found a job working for the famous Harry Miller, builder of Miller race cars and engines. It proved to be the perfect place for him, a fourteen-year-old boy excited and intrigued by the idea of going fast. By the next year, Ed was a riding mechanic on a dirt track car even though the minimum age requirement was twenty-one.

On the Fourth of July in 1921, Ed was at the race track in Hanford, California, for a holiday event in which he raced this Ford. He's shown here (second from right) with his brother (at left in coveralls).

Ed, at age 20, was an avid racer and mechanic, and was dressed in natty style for racing with his waistcoat, goggles, necktie and stroker cap.

One of Ed's creations, a pair of Winfield sidedraft carburetors fitted with downdraft "silencers."

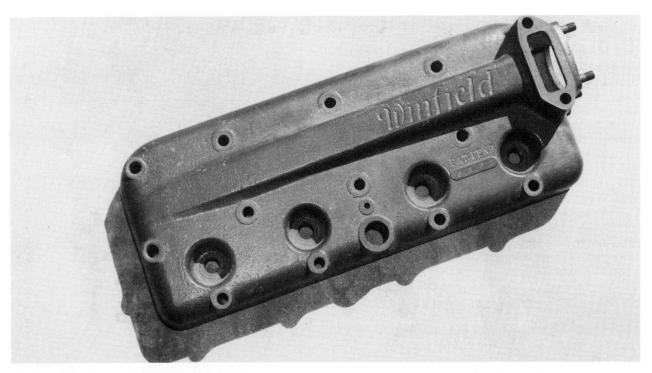

Here is an old Winfield "B" model Crowfoot racing head.

The engine of this Model A roadster is fitted with a Winfield Model-SR downdraft carb.

The Miller facility was a fairyland for Ed, as it had its own engineering staff, foundry and machine shop. His first job was in the carburetor department, where he learned to fix and calibrate the Miller carburetors. Ed soon formulated his own design, but wasn't able to use this knowledge at Miller's, so he knew his time there was finite. He progressed swiftly and was soon assembling race engines. He started learning seriously, and was motivated to go to night school to study science.

The idea of using increased lift and longer-duration cam profiles to improve engine performance developed in Ed's creative mind. On the side, he was building engines for race cars and motorcycles—not stockers, but modifieds with re-ground cams and tricked-out carburetors. Ed had ideas that others were not pursuing and purchased a cam grinding machine.

A man of his own spirit, Ed resigned his job with Miller in 1921 to open his own carburetor business under the name of "The Winfield Carburetor Company." He still studied at night school but during the day he worked on manufacturing a new style of carburetor for production automobiles.

He continued to race at Ascot, building his own cars and equipping them with Winfield carburetors and cams. By 1928, Ed was one of Ascot's champion drivers. His performance improved dramatically, and others took notice.

Ralph DePalma, the famous Miller racer, was among the first to switch to a Winfield carburetor for dirt tracking. By 1925, Winfield's new carburetors had made major inroads into the Indy 500 field.

Ed filed for patents on his carburetors and many of his other engineering ideas, including the Novi racing engine and the fabled "Cheater Cam." He also developed a racing head for Model A Ford engines, which he sold in limited quantities to selected customers.

He demanded privacy as he worked and few were ever able to enter his workshop or, really, his life. His drive for perfection matched his need for privacy. Virtually until the end of his life, Ed continued to personally grind every cam he sold.

Ed Iskenderian told of trying to work for Ed in the late-forties. Isky would stop by the shop regularly, asking all kinds of technical questions about cams. He got the information he asked for, but never the job offer he really wanted. Isky had ordered a Winfield cam for his V-8 90, but Winfield would

Ed Winfield, who was born October 4, 1901, ended up living in Las Vegas for the last twenty years of his life before passing away on April 15, 1982.

open the door of his shop only about six inches to chat or do business. He would take his customer's cash and then vertically pass the cam out through the six-inch gap in the door.

His dealings with customers had a ripple effect. The difficulty of dealing with Ed was a double-header for Isky. Not only could he not get a job working with Winfield, but it took three months to get his cam! The result was that Ed Iskenderian got into the cam business himself.

Ed may well be remembered as one of hot rod's peculiar characters, but his own "need for speed" helped fulfill the speed lust of many early hot rodders and street freaks.

Chapter 32

Gene Winfield

At the busy shop of the "Old Master," Gene Winfield, eager young hot rod and custom car builders learn the trade and hone their skills. But when it's time to chop a top or french the headlights of one of the shop's most important projects, the Master takes over and does the work in his inimitable way. The

Gene is shown with the plug for his 1940 Ford custom. He produced a complete custom fiberglass body and front clip on this chopped, molded, shaved and channeled coupe.

unmarked building in Canoga Park, California, gives passersby no hint that inside is one of hot rodding's greats, handling the torch to cut a top.

As a youth in Modesto, California, Gene and his two brothers got heavily involved with the California hot rod scene, building rods and custom cars while still in high school. When Gene returned from World War II and a tour of duty with the Navy, he opened "Winfield Brothers Service" with his brothers, doing general panel, paint and mechanical work.

Gene went on to open his own shop, "Windy's Custom Shop," in 1947. By 1955, he had opened a new shop called "Winfield's Custom Shop." His cars were hot, and so were his ideas.

Gene's most revered cars are from immediately after the war and early-fifties, a period when he was in his heyday and taking the challenges that twenty-year-olds take "just to see if it can be done."

His education in custom car building was a hands-on exercise of building and selling, selling and building. Hundreds of cars passed through his workshops, and you understand what he's capable of when he casually mentions that they are "going to cut up this '40 Ford coupe, chop three inches off the roof, section the guards and put in a Camaro front end"—as though it was as easy as gassing up the mower to cut the lawn.

He has built cars the way Detroit should have made them when they were first designed, but good design talent develops and matures over a long period.

Eaton Street in Canoga Park, a quiet industrial/residential street in the north end of Los Angeles, is where Gene has his shop today. Its small office understates the importance that Winfield's Custom Shop has had on hot rodders around the world. Gene's cars have always been startling, exotic and brightly colored—such as "Reactor," a hand-beaten, alloy-bodied show car, and "Jade Idol," a 1956 Mercury with blended paint and custom body. He still has many different vehicles in his shop to be restored or to have a major Winfield alteration.

Not many people know of Gene's association with the film industry. When you're leading the field and making the best in California, your talents are in demand. Hollywood was only a freeway away and the movie industry eagerly sought out Gene's talents. Gene built cars and sets for such films as "The Mechanic," "The Hindenburg," "Magnum Force," "Blade Runner," "Sleeper," "Times Are Tough All

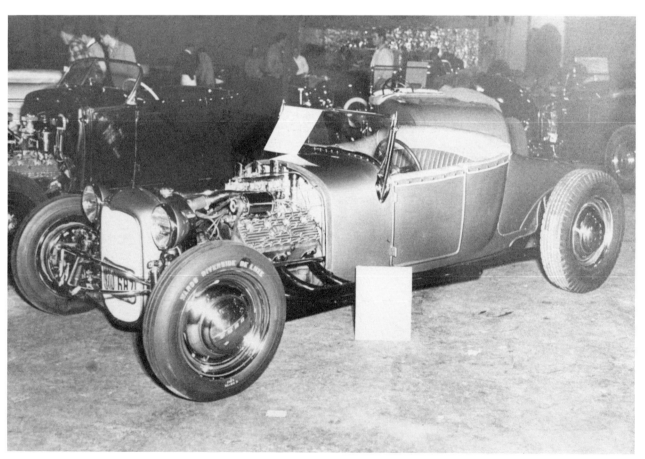

One of Gene's early hot rods was this 1926 T roadster, which featured a deuce grille and was powered by a 24-stud triple Stromberg-fed Mercury flathead V-8. It is shown here on display at the Oakland roadster show.

In the mid-fifties Gene built this 1949 Ford custom with its lake pipes, reverse side scoops, completely new nose, new bumpers and shaved door handles, nose and deck.

The famous "Jade Idol" was one of Gene's creations featuring a slick fade-away color scheme of white and green.

Gene built one of the first Corvette customs, and it featured practically all of the tricks in the book.

Over" and "Last of the Star Fighters." His vehicles have appeared on the TV shows "Mission Impossible," "Mannix," "Star Trek," "Mod Squad" and "Batman."

He has also contributed to some amazing TV commercials, such as Goodyear Tires, where he featured cars driving over meat cleavers, saw blades and fire axes. For Sonoco Gasoline, Gene completely

Ford had Gene build this custom, called the "Pacifica," for its Custom Car Caravan in 1962.

froze a car in a block of ice. The ice was chipped away and an actor stepped in to start the car; it started straight away, of course. Hanover Insurance Trust had Gene construct a car from thirty different cars to emphasize that Hanover would insure "any car," and from Chevrolet came the great challenge (which he met) to cut a car front to rear, completely in half, and make both halves drivable!

Gene made many contacts in the television and movie industry and built such project vehicles as the Bonnie and Clyde car. He also built a convertible Camaro that could be changed into a 1931 Chevy roadster. It was used on the "Dean Martin Show" in a song-and-dance segment in which thirty dancers changed the car from one model to the other while Dean crooned.

Gene's business and reputation grew. He opened a second shop as a closed-door business that built only prototypes of new car designs for Ford and Chrysler. AMT, one of America's leading kit model makers, called on him to open its new speed and custom divisions in Phoenix, Arizona. Gene

closed one of his shops and moved to the new AMT shop, where he built full-scale versions of cars featured in AMT model kits.

Gene will accept any challenge: models, prototypes, alloy bodies, chop tops and cars built from photos. He always says, "Yes, I can build that for you," and then proceeds to do so.

Other projects have included Cadillac pickups and station wagons, stretched limos and convertible conversions. If you want something different, Gene's probably already done it. As the movie industry knows, Gene is a source of imaginative ideas and a producer of "auto exotica."

Gene took time out some years ago to review his life and decided to close his regular panel and body conversion workshop. He shut his door to the everyday humdrum of a panel man. Now, he does two types of work: for the film industry and on his true love, forties and fifties custom cars.

His pet project is a 1947 Ford coupe with a chopped top, molded fenders and internally hinged trunk and doors. For this coupe, Gene has made a

This was a beauty: the famous split car, which consisted of two working halves of an Impala. It was created for use in a commercial. The car was filmed going down the road, *then splitting in two, with both halves continuing to cruise along.*

For "The Dean Martin Show," Gene built this car which could be transformed in minutes from a 1968 Camaro to a

1932 Chevrolet roadster. The change was made by switching fiberglass bodies and substituting fake wheels.

fiberglass replica body, nose to tail, interior and floor. This is the first fiberglass replica leadsled. It is quite a revolution because it's almost impossible to find late-forties coupes and it's so expensive to chop in metal. To add to this new product, Gene has a full line of fiberglass body parts for custom and stock cars, and is developing new products for early customs.

For his own pleasure, he is slowly building a 1917 T roadster. Slowly is the word, because he started this car in 1958—but he's getting there. So far, he has built a tube frame with a front blower and two

Predator carburetors onto a Ford V–8. The Potvin blower drives straight off the crankshaft with a twin magneto unit in between, and the manifold runs out the side, up over the hood and into the top of the motor. It's a most unusual combination and when it is finished, Gene's T roadster will be another prize winner for looks and engineering.

You can visit him but don't expect to find a sign out front. His low, beige building looks like a warehouse, not the home of one of the world's most creative car builders. That's just the way Gene likes it.

We put it all together. The AnyCar Loan.

'29 Hudson
'73 Triumph
'71 Continental
'73 Toyota
'71 Mach I
'58 Volvo
'70 Pontiac
'61 Imperial
'66 Corvette
'61 Valiant
'68 Ford
'73 Plymouth
'70 Mustang
'67 Volkswagen
'69 Toronado
'70 Catalina
'54 Chrysler
'69 Cadillac
'73 Mercedes

Get any car—new, used, sporty or sensible—with 180 days to shop around for the best deal.

The "AnyCar" was a project Gene undertook on behalf of a financial company that wanted to show how versatile it was when it came to car loans.

Gene "Windy" Winfield

Index